withdrawn

D1506288

THE FLORIDA KEYS

A History of the Pioneers

FLORIDA'S
THROUGH
ITS
PLACES
HISTORY

THE FLORIDA KEYS

A History of the Pioneers

John Viele

FLORIDA'S
THROUGH
ITS
PLACES
HISTORY

 PINEAPPLE PRESS, INC.
Sarasota, Florida

Copyright © 1996 by John Viele

Inquiries should be addressed to:
Pineapple Press, Inc.
P.O. Box 3899
Sarasota, Florida 34230-3899

LIBRARY OF CONGRESS
CATALOGING IN PUBLICATION DATA

Viele, John, 1923-
      The Florida keys : a history of the pioneers / John Viele. – 1st ed.
          p.   cm. – (Florida's history through its places)
      Includes bibliographical references and index.
      ISBN 1-56164-101-4 (alk. paper)
      1. Florida Keys (Fla.)–History. 2. Florida Keys (Fla.)–Social life and customs.
3. Florida Keys (Fla.)–Biography. I. Title. II. Series.
F317.M7V54 1996
975.9'41–dc20   95-50036
                                                CIP

First Edition
10 9 8 7 6 5 4 3 2

Design by Carol Tornatore
Printed and bound by Quebecor/Fairfield, Fairfield, Pennsylvania

To Pam, my wife,

whose love, encouragement, and help

brought this work to fruition

Contents

Acknowledgments

*I*n researching and writing this book, I have received valuable assistance from many individuals and organizations, but the following persons are particularly deserving of my thanks. Jim Miller, a former *Washington Post* editor and instructor in journalism at the Florida Keys Community College, helped me believe I really could write. Dan Gallagher, a true friend, devoted many hours to reviewing my work and helping me polish my writing skills. Gail Swanson, a dedicated Keys history researcher, shared the results of her search for Keys history before 1800. Tom Hambright, director of the Florida History Department at Monroe County Public Library, reviewed the text for historical accuracy and, together with his assistant, Lynda Hambright, helped me locate sources in the library's extensive collection. Jim Clupper, director of the Helen Wadley Branch Library of Monroe County and Keys historian, provided much useful information from sources he has discovered. Jerry Wilkinson, president of the Historical Preservation Society of the Upper Keys, kindly allowed me to search through his extensive photographic collection for potential illustrations. Ray Blazevic, who has amassed a treasure trove of Keys history, combed his collection of old maps to find ones I was looking for. Jack Lane, professor of history at Rollins College, offered valuable comments on the manuscript from a professional historian's point of view.

I am indebted to the following individuals for their contributions of information, documents, and photographs which helped to bring certain Keys pioneers to life.

To Joseph Whalton, great-great-grandson of Capt. John Whalton, and his wife Sally Whalton for source documents which contributed significant information to the story "John Whalton – Lone Sentinel on the Reef." Sally Whalton is also due my thanks for having the foresight to interview her Uncle Pete Chase and record his memories of his experiences on Sugarloaf Key helping his father in the attempt to grow sponges commercially.

To Eugene R. Lytton Sr., former mayor of Monroe County, for his research into the life of Temple Pent Sr. which he documented in a booklet, "The Honorable Squire Pent Sr."

To Patricia Warren for her research, source documents, and photogaphs which helped me write the story of her great grandfather, Nicholas Matcovich.

To Mary and George Bow for sharing with me family papers and memories of their grandmother, Lily Lawrence Bow.

To Fred Key for telling me the story of his boyhood days on Little Pine Key where his family grew tomatoes.

To Lillian Spencer Roberts for relating to me her memories of the hardships she suffered as a young girl on Key Largo.

To Mary Johnson, Fred Johnson Jr., and Sylvia Johnson Torres for recounting their memories of their parents, Fred and Mary Johnson, and their youthful experiences at Perky on Sugarloaf Key.

Also, I should not forget to thank Bob Cummings for his creative drawings of Keys natives, Naya Rydzewski for her artistic recreation of the attack on the schooner *Mary*, Nancy Jameson and David Harrison Wright for permission to use David's painting of the killing of Captain Whalton, and Wright and Joan Langley for reviewing my work and offering valuable suggestions for sources of Keys history.

Introduction

*M*any of these stories of Florida Keys settlers originally appeared in columns in the *Island Navigator* newspaper and articles in *Florida Keys Magazine*. Together with overviews of the periods in which the settlers lived, these tales bring to life the history of the unique semitropical islands that are the Florida Keys.

From Native Americans to Bahamian immigrants, from turtle hunters to wreck salvagers, and from sponge gatherers to pineapple planters, the rural Keys settlers struggled in different ways to turn the natural bounties of the Keys into a living or a profit. Except for the Native Americans, few succeeded. Most fought the heat, the mosquitoes, the lack of fresh water, and the isolation for a few years and then left or died.

These stories are not about the lawyers, merchants, and ship captains who made Key West, for a time, one of the richest cities per capita in the United States. They are about the little-known men and women who beached their boats on isolated Keys and struggled through the mangroves to begin new lives in a strange and often hostile semitropical wilderness.

Few of the Keys pioneers knew how to read or write, or, if they did, never had the time to pen diaries or letters. Most of what we know about them comes from more educated travelers who visited the Keys, from government reports and records, and from a few oral histories.

Modern residents and visitors are connected to the mainland by highway, pipeline, and electric umbilical cords and insulated from the realities of the Keys environment by air conditioners and mosquito sprays. They may have difficulty transposing themselves mentally into the shoes of these pioneers, but they can hardly fail to appreciate the courage, determination, and ingenuity with which yesteryears' settlers faced life in the Florida Keys.

xi

THE FLORIDA KEYS

A History of the Pioneers

Chapter 1

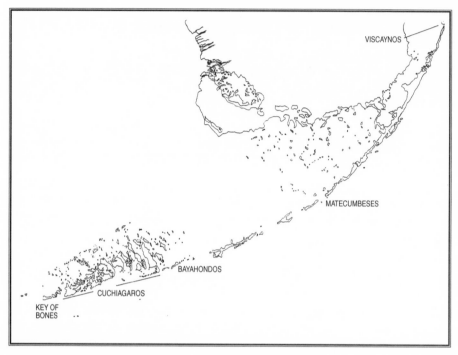

Native American groups in the Keys in the seventeenth century

THEY WERE HERE FIRST

(3000 B.C. – A.D. 1763)

*S*ome archaeologists believe Native Americans began occupying the Keys as early as 3000 B.C. A site on Key Largo has been radiocarbon dated at 1000 B.C. Archaeological evidence indicates that around A.D. 100, the native population of the Keys began to increase significantly, eventually reaching between 500 and 1,000 inhabitants. For the next 1,400 years, these original settlers of the Keys thrived on the natural bounties of the islands and the sea around them. Then, beginning in the early 1500s, the Europeans – explorers, slave hunters, castaways, fishermen, soldiers, and missionaries – arrived. In the short space of 250 years the Keys natives were gone, wiped out by the white man's swords, guns, disease, and rum; by his determination to convert them to Christianity; and, finally, by his setting one Indian nation against another.

There are conflicting opinions among archaeologists as to whether the aboriginal natives of the Keys were a branch of the Calusa, a warlike people living on Florida's southwest coast or a branch of the Tequesta, a more peaceful tribe centered around the mouth of the Miami River. But, it is true that, in at least one period in their history, the Keys natives were subject to the Calusa and paid them tribute in the form of captured castaways and gold and silver from wrecks.

3

What were the Keys natives like, and how did they live? Our earliest glimpse is as they were approximately fifty years after Columbus's first voyage. A thirteen-year-old boy, Hernando d'Escalante Fontaneda, was on his way to Spain from Cartagena when his ship was wrecked somewhere in the Keys. The survivors were captured by the natives; those who were not immediately killed were made slaves. Fontaneda's life was spared and he lived among various South Florida Native American tribes for seventeen years.

Through Fontaneda's eyes we learn that the Keys natives were large in stature and the women well-proportioned and of good appearance. "To cover their shame," the men wore a loincloth of woven palm and the women wore an early version of the miniskirt made of Spanish moss.

The natives of the Keys were hunter-gatherers and did not practice any form of agriculture. Their staple foods from the sea were fish, turtle, lobster, shellfish, seals, and manatee. The latter were reserved for the chiefs and other bigwigs. Described in a Spanish document as "great archers and spear throwers," they hunted deer and raccoon for meat. They also subsisted on wild fruits such as sea grapes, palm berries, and cocoplums.

Archaeological digs reveal that shells were the principal implements of everyday life. The sharp lips of conch shells were used as gouges, scrapers, and ax heads. A whole shell with holes cut in it for a stick handle served as a hammer, hatchet, or club. The center columns of shells became awls or drills. Shells were also important aids to cooking and eating when used as cups, saucers, dippers, and spoons.

The original natives of the Keys lived in small groups, each under the leadership of a chief. Spanish documents refer to a Chief of the Key of Bones (Key West) and a Chief of the Matecumbeses. Other tribal groupings mentioned were the Viscaynos (Biscayne Bay area), the Bayahondos (Bahia Honda area), and the Cuchiagaros (Lower Keys). Evidence of Native American occupation has been found on nearly all the larger Keys.

There are no descriptions of their habitations other than references to "huts." Archaeologists speculate that these were made of tree branches lashed together with vines and covered with roofs of thatched palm.

Although firsthand accounts of Keys natives' religious practices are unavailable, it is probably safe to assume that they were similar to those of

Keys natives were hunter-gatherers (drawing by Robert Cummings)

other South Florida tribes. Each group had a head priest who served as medicine man, prophet, intermediary with the gods, and leader of religious rites. A large rock mound found on Key Largo, over 100 feet long and 15 feet high, is believed to have been built for holding religious ceremonies.

As contact with Europeans increased during the 1500s, the Keys natives' attitude changed from awe and fear to hostility. Castaways could expect to be killed or turned over to the bloodthirsty Calusa as tribute. Many of the latter were sacrificed in religious ceremonies. All this changed when Spanish fishermen from Cuba discovered the prolific fishing grounds of the Keys. With gifts of trinkets, bright-colored cloth, knives, and, most effective of all, rum, they gradually won the Keys natives' friendship. As an example of this, when the Spanish frigate *Nuestra Senora del Rosario* grounded off the Matecumbe Keys in 1605, the natives helped free the vessel and gave the crew fresh water, fish, and wood.

By the time of the loss of the Spanish treasure fleet in the hurricane of 1622, Keys natives had been plundering wrecks for over 100 years and had learned how to dive to obtain treasures they could not otherwise reach. During the Spanish salvage operations beginning in 1628, Keys natives were employed as salvage divers and helped recover a large number of silver bars and coins.

In addition to the fishing craft, other Spanish vessels began to visit the Keys and the southwest coast of Florida to trade with the natives. Eventually, the natives were no longer content to wait for the arrival of Spanish vessels. Demonstrating remarkable seamanship and daring, they began crossing the Florida Straits in their own dugout canoes. By the late 1690s, South Florida natives were arriving at Havana regularly with cargoes of fish, ambergris, tree bark, fruits, and animal pelts which they sold or traded for rum, knives, hatchets, fishhooks, clothing, trinkets, and so forth. They also brought live cardinal birds which were highly prized by Spanish seamen and sold for ten pesos apiece.

By the early 1700s, the few Keys natives who had managed to survive white mens' swords, rum, and diseases had acquired a thin veneer of Spanish culture. Most of the adult men spoke a little Spanish and had adopted Spanish names. Their leaders used Spanish titles such as "captain-general," "bishop," and "king." Although many had been baptized in Havana and professed to be Catholics, they still clung to their old religious beliefs and customs. Some worked for the Spanish fishermen, helping them catch and cure fish in exchange for rum. Others salvaged wrecks or made trading voyages to Havana.

The early 1700s were also the beginning of raids into Florida by various native tribes north of the border. Supported by and sometimes led by the British, these raiding parties destroyed the Spanish missions, killed many of the original Florida natives, and carried many more off into slavery on the plantations. As a result of the raids, groups of South Florida natives, including those from the Keys, fled to Cuba, where, trapped in an alien environment, most of them died.

The last of these migrations occurred in the 1750s and opening years of the 1760s and probably included the last of the Keys natives. When, in 1763, Florida was ceded to England, there were, according to one source, about eighty families of Calusa natives who had taken refuge on Key West and Key Vaca. The departing Spanish took the Calusa with them to Cuba, and the Keys were then uninhabited.

Although there were many encounters between Europeans and the Keys natives, there are very few reports of their experiences. This is understandable because many of the Europeans did not survive the meetings and those who did were for the most part sailors or fishermen who could neither read nor write. Among the few accounts that exist, only one has been found which actually describes Keys natives as individuals. It comes from the pen of a French priest who was shipwrecked in the Keys in 1722. His narrative provides a rare snapshot of a band of Keys natives as they appeared after 200 years of contact with the Spanish.

Don Diego — "King" of the Keys Natives

The captain thought they should steer more to the east but the pilot, with a single passage through the Straits of Florida to his credit, insisted a more northerly course was correct. With land in sight, the lookout at the masthead said the water was turning white, but the officers on deck laughed at him. Shortly thereafter, the French sailing ship *Adour*, bound in 1722 for Santo Domingo from Biloxi, Mississippi, struck the Florida Reef.

Father Pierre F. X. de Charlevoix, king's emissary to explore New France, shipwrecked in Keys in 1722 (de Charlevoix, P. F. X., *History and General Description of New France*)

The following morning, while the crew made halfhearted, ineffectual attempts to refloat the ship, the passengers were ferried to the nearest key, about five miles distant. Among the passengers was a French priest, Pierre de Charlevoix, returning from a mission to survey French territory in North America and report his findings to the king. The priest recorded his experiences in a journal which was subsequently published.

As the boats neared the shore of a low-lying, bush-covered key, a large band of natives appeared carrying bows and arrows. Their skin was very red, redder than that of any other Native Americans Charlevoix had encountered in his travels, and they wore only palm leaves or pieces of bark to cover their privates.

The boats stopped short of the shore. Seeing the Frenchmen were afraid to land, the natives laid down their weapons and waded out into the water. In Spanish, they asked if their visitors were English. The passengers replied that they were French and allies of the Spanish. Obviously pleased to hear this, the natives invited them to land, assuring them that they would be perfectly safe on the island.

The leader of the natives said his name was Don Antonio. Not only did he speak Spanish reasonably well, but he also boasted that he was a *caballero* (Spanish gentleman), one of the most distinguished in his tribe. He told Charlevoix that nearly all of the people of his village had been baptized as Catholics in Havana and that they voyaged there once a year. These voyages were made in dugout canoes described as "small, very flat pirogues, in which we [Frenchmen] should hardly trust ourselves across the Seine at Paris."

Don Antonio said that they had a "king" whose name was Don Diego and that he would come to visit them the next day. He asked the Frenchmen what they intended to do. When they replied that they would try to get to St. Augustine, he offered to guide them there.

It soon became apparent from the natives' behavior that their main interest was in seeing what they could get from the Frenchmen by begging or stealing. Don Antonio asked Charlevoix for his "girdle" (possibly a sash around his waist). Although the priest said no, Don Antonio continued to demand that it be given to him.

There is insufficient information in the priest's journal to determine where the ship hit the reef. The key they landed on was described as being about nine miles in circumference with a soil of sand and broken coral, and possessing neither trees nor four-footed animals. There were other islands nearby, the closest and smallest of which was the site of the natives' "cabins." The natives subsisted entirely on seafood. Charlevoix concluded that the only reason they remained on these barren islands was to plunder wrecks.

A week passed before the natives' king, Don Diego, arrived. In the meantime, the ship's crew had been occupied with making the boats ready to leave. The king, a young man of short stature, was less than impressive. He wore a few rags which were "not worth picking off a dunghill" and a headband, the only item of apparel that distinguished him from his subjects. His wife, the queen, was a well-shaped, attractive young woman who was "decently clothed for an Indian."

When questioned about Don Antonio's offer to guide them to St. Augustine, Don Diego said that he would do all within his power to help them. To further persuade him in their favor, Charlevoix presented him with a shirt which he accepted with profuse thanks.

The next day, the king arrived wearing the shirt, which hung down to his heels, over his rags. Although he appeared ridiculous to the Frenchmen, he was quite pleased with his attire. He then explained that he was not the absolute ruler of his people, but rather a sort of sub-chief under the authority of a supreme chief who lived far away (possibly the chief of the Calusa or the Tequesta). Nevertheless, he was the unquestioned ruler of his own village. Don Antonio, who was twice the king's size and age, told

9

Charlevoix that the king had severely beaten him for getting drunk on some spirits left on board the wrecked ship.

The following day, Don Diego invited himself to dinner with the Frenchmen. He was offered meat, but refused it, eating instead some fish he had given the castaways the previous day. The king said that, after much consideration, he had decided against allowing Don Antonio to guide them to St. Augustine because there were many tribes along the way with whom he was at war. Among others, he may have been referring to the Yamasees from South Carolina who, aided and led by the English, had been raiding Florida tribes and carrying away natives for sale into slavery.

Twelve days after the wreck, the Frenchmen sailed away in their boats. One group reached Havana while the other, with Charlevoix aboard, after many adventures, eventually succeeded in reaching Biloxi.

"The next day, the king arrived wearing the shirt, which hung down to his heels, over his rags." (drawing by Robert Cummings)

Don Diego did not disappear from the pages of history. In 1732, ten years after meeting Charlevoix, he and thirteen of his "first rank" followers were brought to Havana for an audience with the Governor of Cuba. The governor explained that the King of Spain wished the Keys natives to move to Cuba so that they could be instructed in the faith and baptized. Afterwards they would be given land along the coast where they could farm and fish. Cacique (chief) Don Diego, as the Spanish called him, expressed great pleasure with the offer and promised to return to the Keys and bring back his people.

Two ships carried the Cacique and his retinue back to the Keys. For three days, a large gathering of natives feasted and drank rum on board the ships. But, on the morning of the fourth day, the Spanish awoke to find that all of them, including Don Diego, had disappeared.

Don Diego's name also appears in a letter from the Governor of Florida at St. Augustine to the Governor of Cuba at Havana written in 1740. Because St. Augustine was blockaded by English ships, the governor sent the letter by canoe. He instructed the Spaniard and two Indians who manned the canoe to go to the Keys and try to find a Spanish fishing vessel to take them to Havana. Failing that, they were to look for Cacique Don Diego and ask for his help.

With that letter, Don Diego's name disappears from documents in the Spanish archives. It is possible, if he survived the Creek and Uchise raids in the 1740s and '50s, that he came to Cuba with one of the last groups of native refugees in 1761. Most of these exiles died soon after leaving their home in the Keys.

Chapter 2

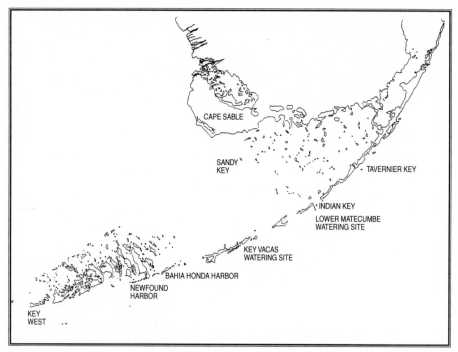

Harbors and watering sites frequented by wreckers and fishermen
in the late 1700s and early 1800s

NO MAN'S LAND

(1764 – 1819)

*F*rom the time the last natives in the Keys were taken to Cuba in 1763 until the first Americans settled at Key West in 1819, a period of fifty-six years, the Keys were devoid of permanent settlements, but certainly not deserted. For the first twenty years, the Keys were nominally English territory and for the last thirty-six, Spanish, but neither the English nor the Spanish authorities maintained any effective control over the islands.

In fact, the authorities at Havana never considered that the Keys had left their dominion. They referred to them as the "Norte de Havana," and continued to issue licenses to Cuban fishing vessels to go to the Keys even while they were English territory. Each year from August to March, fleets of some thirty Cuban fishing smacks would fish the Keys and the southwest coast of Florida and would salt and dry their catches on shore.

The Cubans were not alone in the Keys. Even before Florida was ceded to England, Bahamian vessels were coming to the Keys to hunt turtle, cut timber, and salvage wrecks. The Spanish made no effort to stop them. When the fear of attack by the natives was removed, the Bahamians came in greater numbers. In 1764, a Cuban official on his way to confer with the British governor at St. Augustine observed fourteen Bahamian vessels in the Keys.

The British governor was directed to put a stop to the intrusion of Cuban vessels because it was feared that their presence might threaten British control of Florida. But the governor had no means to stop the Cubans and was forced to accept the situation. In 1766, he urged that a post or settlement be established at Key West, saying that it was ideally situated for trade with Havana in time of peace and strategically advantageous in time of war, but nothing came of his plea.

The governor was also upset that the Bahamians, even though they were English subjects, were taking mahogany and other valuable hardwoods from his territory. He sent a ship to the Keys to warn them to stop, but it had little effect. As early as 1769, it was reported that most of the valuable timber in the Keys had been cut down.

The principal harbors used by the Cuban and Bahamian vessels were Key West, Newfound (Big Pine Key), Bahia Honda, Indian Key, and Tavernier Key. Staying in the Keys for weeks or months at a time, the crews supplemented their stores of dry biscuit and barreled pork by fishing and hunting. Water was obtained from natural sinkholes. The watering place at the western end of Key Vacas was described as "a particularly large one . . .

Ship's watering site at Key West first described by surveyor Bernard Romans in 1769 (reproduction of 1832 drawing by George Lehman, courtesy of Monroe County Public Library)

where the water never fails." At Lower Matecumbe there were "five natural wells . . . constantly full of excellent water." Bernard Romans, a British surveyor who explored the Keys in 1769, wrote that at Key West there was "a well or pond of excellent water round which a low kind of stone wall is placed . . . the trees are marked with many names."

Because the reefs posed such a serious danger to ships, development of accurate charts received high priority. The work of Bernard Romans was continued by the English surveyor George Gauld in the early 1770s. But the arrival of American privateers in the Keys at the beginning of the Revolutionary War forced him to discontinue his survey before it was finished. Gauld's charts and sailing directions were the standard for navigation of the Keys until American surveys were begun some seventy-five years later.

With the end of the Revolutionary War in 1783, Florida reverted to Spain, but the change in ownership did nothing to change the situation in the Keys. Cuban fishermen and Bahamian wreckers continued to ply the Keys in pursuit of their trades. In the absence of any effective control by Spanish authorities, the Keys gradually became havens for smugglers and privateers. The latter group were not particular about whose flag unarmed merchantmen flew.

A Cuban official in 1790 reported the existence of a Bahamian settlement in the upper Keys which was probably a temporary camp set up by the turtlers and wreckers. There are also reports of people settling in the Keys as early as 1806 and 1807, but who they were and how long they stayed is not known.

In the early 1800s, the number of Bahamian vessels in the Keys continued to increase. In 1806, it was reported that twenty-eight to thirty wreckers came to the Keys from the Bahamas each year. In 1822, the governor of the territory of Florida estimated that there were almost forty. The value of the wrecking business to the Bahamian government in court fees and customs duty on salvaged goods was reported to be £15,000 annually.

After the end of the War of 1812, New England fishermen, particularly from Mystic, Connecticut, began coming to the Keys in the winter to fish for the Havana market and to salvage wrecks. These New Englanders were among the first settlers of Key West; it is even reported that a group from Mystic started a short-lived settlement on Key Vaca in 1818.

The following tale, taken from the journal of Col. David Fanning, illustrates the variety of characters, good and bad, one might have encountered in the Florida Keys in the late 1700s.

Colonel Fanning – Trying Times in the Keys

A small flotilla of open boats set sail from Mosquito Inlet (near modern-day Daytona Beach) on March 20, 1784. On board were seven families of American loyalists who had fled to Florida at the end of the Revolutionary War. With the return of Florida to Spain by the terms of the Treaty of Paris, the English settlers there were forced to find new homes.

The boats headed south along the Florida coast; their final destination: Fort Natchez on the Mississippi River, 1,400 miles away. Their leader was Col. David Fanning, age twenty-nine, who had been a daring commander of Loyalist partisans in the south during the war. His exploits included the capture of the capital of North Carolina and numerous escapes from imprisonment by the rebels.

Accompanying Fanning were his eighteen-year-old pregnant wife; two young slaves, a male and a female; and an eighteen-year-old white man. They were in two boats together with all the personal property they could carry. It appears that they had no chart and very little knowledge of what lay ahead of them. They only knew that, if they continued to follow the coastline after leaving the Florida Keys, they would eventually reach the mouth of the Mississippi. Beyond Mosquito Inlet, there was not another white settlement until they reached Pensacola. Because they could carry only a small amount of food and water on board, they would have to stop often to find water and to hunt, fish, and gather nuts and berries.

On their way down the east coast, the Fannings became separated from the rest of the boats. They reached the vicinity of Key West about a month after leaving Mosquito Inlet. Here they met a Spanish schooner, and the colonel went aboard to talk to her crew. Fanning could not speak Spanish, and the crew could not speak English. But as it happened, there were some Creeks on board. Before the Revolution, Fanning had been an Indian trader and knew how to speak Creek. Fanning told the Creeks he was bound for the Mississippi. They advised him that he was on the edge of the Gulf of Mexico and that it was a three-day sail over open water to the mainland. The Spanish sailors understood what Fanning was saying and, in Creek, warned him that six or seven English families from St. Augustine had been killed by the natives some time ago while crossing the Bay of Tompay (Tampa Bay). Hearing this, Fanning decided to encamp at Key West and consider his next move.

For the next fifteen days, the wind blew at or near gale force. While waiting for calmer weather, Fanning visited another Spanish schooner which had taken shelter in the harbor. Using the Creek language again, Fanning obtained information on navigating the Keys and was once more warned of the dangers of trying to sail up the west coast of Florida.

The stories of the killings by the natives so frightened the young man traveling with Fanning that he transferred aboard the schooner, preferring a visit to Cuba to a voyage through hostile territory. The night before the schooner left, some of her crew slipped ashore and, while the Fannings slept, stole most of their clothes and bedding.

Still determined to reach the Mississippi and better informed on the geography of the Keys, Fanning sailed back up the Keys to Key Vaca. From there he headed due north and, after an eight-hour sail, reached Sandy Key, about six miles southeast of Cape Sable.

The next day, while approaching Cape Sable, Fanning met a small schooner from New Providence (Nassau today) on a turtle-hunting voyage. Now that he was on the edge of the hostile natives' territory, Fanning began to have second thoughts about continuing on. He asked the captain, an unprincipled Italian named Baptist, if he would carry his people and his property to New Providence. At first, Baptist said he could not answer until he had loaded his turtles. The next day he said yes, he would do it for $200. Fanning protested the price as exorbitant, another day passed, and the captain lowered it to $150. Fanning said it was still more than he had and, with the help of his wife and the two slaves, sailed his two boats into shore.

On the fourth day after meeting the schooner, Fanning saw two men seize his slave girl and carry her out to the schooner which had been moved close to shore to mend the turtle nets. About a half hour later, he saw the captain and another seaman carry her ashore and into the woods.

Fanning, who had remained out of sight, suspected their next move might be to kill him. With only one powder charge left for his gun, he decided his best course would be the boldest one. When the captain and the seaman emerged from the woods, he advanced toward them. Both men started to go back into the woods, but Fanning ran and caught up with the seaman before he disappeared. The seaman denied any knowledge of the girl's whereabouts and told Fanning he better ask the captain about her.

A little while later as Fanning was returning to his boats, he looked back and saw Baptist standing on the beach with a gun over his arm. Fanning turned and started walking towards him. As he drew near, he saw the captain's gun was cocked. Fanning told him to uncock it and tell him what he had done with his slave girl. Baptist refused to uncock the gun and denied knowing anything about the girl.

A lengthy, heated discussion ensued. In the course of it, the captain said even if he did have the girl, he would keep her because he had lost a slave boy that cost him $800 and he needed to make some money before he went back to New Providence. Fanning, realizing he had nothing to bargain with, finally agreed to give him $150 but not his slave girl. He thought that when they got to New Providence, with the help of acquaintances there, he would be able to get the outrageous price reduced.

The next day, Fanning loaded his property aboard the schooner. His wife found the slave girl in the hold, hidden among some sails and stripped of her clothing. What happened to the girl while she was in the clutches of the crew is not difficult to imagine, but Fanning does not say, probably because he did not think the sufferings of a slave worthy of mention.

The schooner sailed off to load turtles from a turtle crawl (pen) and to get wood and water for the return trip. During the twenty days she was gone, the Fannings took their boats across to the mainland and took shelter in the lee of Cape Sable.

When the schooner returned, the Fannings went out to meet her in their smaller boat leaving the large boat at Cape Sable. Baptist presented Fanning with a promissory note for $200 rather than the $150 agreed on. Fanning said he would die before he signed, and the captain ordered him to get in his boat and leave. Fanning protested that his small boat would not hold a fourth of his property, which was already on board the schooner. By this time, Fanning's wife was in tears and begged him to accept the captain's demands lest they meet a worse fate if they were thrown back in their boats. Realizing that they would sustain an even greater loss if forced to leave, Fanning told the captain he would sign the note.

The schooner then sailed to New (Upper) Matecumbe. Along the way, the captain accused Fanning of planning to have him hung when they got to New Providence and said were it not for Fanning's wife, he would have heaved him overboard.

Three schooners from New Providence arrived at Matecumbe about two weeks later. One of the captains came aboard Baptist's schooner and was outraged when Fanning told him how he had been treated. He told Fanning not only was it contrary to the laws of New Providence to coerce a person in distress in such a way, but it was a captain's duty to render every assistance possible. All three captains offered to help, and the Fannings transferred to one of the schooners that was headed back to New Providence.

After nearly three months in the Keys, most of it in the clutches of the nefarious Baptist, the Fannings finally reached New Providence in mid-July. Upon arrival, the Bahamian captain would accept no more than $20 for the passage. Eventually, the Fannings settled in Canada.

Chapter 3

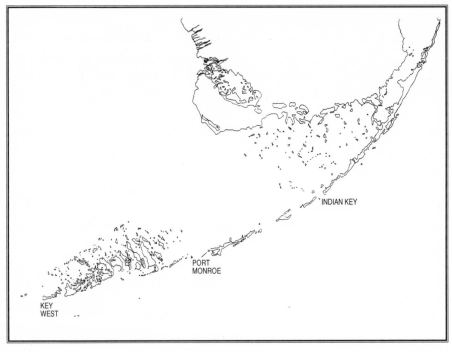

First American settlements in the Keys

AMERICAN OCCUPATION BEGINS

(1820 – 1835)

*W*hen the treaty transferring Florida to the United States was drawn in 1819, according to a Nassau newspaper, several American settlers came to Key West to salvage wrecks. But when John Simonton purchased the island from Juan Salas in January 1822, he stated there was "no living person" on the island; 1822 is the generally accepted date for the original settlement of Key West. A month after Simonton's purchase, Lt. M. C. Perry USN, in command of the U.S. Schooner *Shark*, took formal possession of the island for the United States in the presence of a few recently arrived settlers.

Key West was selected as the site of the first permanent American settlement in the Keys primarily because of its excellent harbor, the best in the Keys. While wrecking was the major attraction, other considerations were the island's position astride major sea-trade routes, the proximity of Cuban markets, the prolific fishing grounds, and the potential for salt manufacture from the natural salt ponds.

The U.S. Navy also quickly recognized the strategic advantages of Key West. The island was perfectly situated to guard the gateway to the U.S. Gulf coast and to serve as a base to protect shipping in the Gulf of

21

Mexico and the Caribbean. The harbor was sufficiently deep to accommodate the Navy's largest ships, sailing vessels could enter and leave the harbor with ease in the prevailing winds, there was access to the Gulf of Mexico and the Florida Straits for all but the largest ships, and there were adequate supplies of wood and fresh water.

Driven by the profits from the wrecking business, Key West grew steadily in the 1820s and '30s. Not only mariners, but merchants, lawyers, artisans, and laborers were attracted to the town. By 1830, the population was 517, including whites, free blacks, and slaves. The free blacks were employed principally as laborers and seamen. The slaves were mostly domestic servants owned by the wealthier merchants and wrecking captains.

Wrecking was the mainstay of the economy. Nearly every citizen derived his living in some way or another from the business, but the principal benefactors were a few merchants. They owned the wharves, warehouses, chandleries, and ship-repair facilities as well as a number of their own wrecking vessels. In 1835, there were twenty good-sized wrecking vessels patrolling the reef, plus a number of smaller craft, mostly fishermen, all of whom had wrecking licenses. With the establishment of a Federal Superior Court in Key West in 1828, the business became well regulated.

Fishing and port operations provided important secondary sources of employment and income. In the 1830s, export of live fish, chiefly to Havana, amounted to between $15,000 and $20,000 annually. By 1834, maritime traffic had increased to the point that, on the average, one vessel entered the harbor and another left nearly every day. Approximately 75 percent of all imports and exports to the Territory of Florida passed through the port of Key West. Two other industries, cigar making and salt manufacture, made their first appearance in the 1830s, but did not contribute significantly to the economy until later years.

When Commodore David Porter established the headquarters of his antipiracy squadron at Key West in 1823, the leading citizens were overjoyed, thinking it would provide another boost to the local economy. Their happiness was short-lived. Porter maintained that the island and everyone on it were subordinate to the needs of the Navy and established himself as an autocratic ruler. His sailors seized the citizens' firewood and killed their

Wreckers at work (*Harper's New Monthly Magazine* Vol. 18, 1858/59, courtesy of Florida State Archives)

livestock without compensation. Porter prohibited the sale of land and the occupation of new land without his approval. In effect, he declared martial law. When he departed at the end of 1824, the citizens breathed a sigh of relief. The following year, because of yellow fever epidemics, the Navy moved the base to Pensacola.

One of the most significant events in Key West's opening years was its designation as a U.S. port of entry and the establishment of a customs house and a collector of customs. This meant that salvaged cargoes could be legally entered at Key West instead of at the next nearest port of entry – St. Augustine, some 400 miles distant. It also allowed Key West to function as a transshipment port for foreign cargoes, particularly those from Cuba.

While Key West enjoyed all the advantages previously mentioned, it had one disadvantage as a wrecking center. It was remote from the sections of the reef that had the highest incidence of wrecks. The reefs off the upper

Keys – Carysfort Reef in particular – were the most hazardous to shipping and were at least two or three days' sail upwind from Key West. This geographical situation was the principal reason why two other Keys settlements were established not long after Key West was founded.

The first outlying settlement was made on Knight (or Knight's) Key at the western end of Key Vaca in November 1822, just nine months after the U.S. flag was raised at Key West. Its founder, Joshua Appleby, a wrecking captain with dreams of developing a thriving maritime business, named it Port Monroe. The story of his ill-fated attempts to enrich himself through collusion with a South American privateer follows later in this chapter. After he left Knight Key in 1825, the settlement was gradually abandoned until, in 1837, only one house remained.

Appleby was also responsible for the start of the second outlying Keys settlement. In 1824, he and a partner named Snyder decided to open a store on Indian Key to trade with the wreckers as well as the settlers and Indians on the southern mainland. Indian Key was a popular rendezvous of the wreckers because of its central location along the reef and the availability of fresh water from nearby Lower Matecumbe Key. It was also far less subject to mosquito invasions than the larger keys. In April 1824, Silas Fletcher, an employee of Appleby at Knight Key, sailed to Indian Key with a stock of goods and orders to build and manage a store.

The following year, Fletcher's wife and children joined him on the eleven-acre island. Soon, other wreckers and turtlers brought their families to live there. By 1829, there were enough women – about a dozen – to hold a "ball" on the piazza of the island's largest building. Around 1830, an enterprising but unscrupulous wrecking captain named Jacob Housman took up residence and proceeded to take over the island as his own private empire. His story, which is also the story of the rise and fall of Indian Key, is told in Chapter 4.

In the late 1820s and early 1830s, as Port Monroe faded from existence, a few wreckers and some immigrants from the Bahamas began settling on the eastern end of Key Vaca, where there was a good supply of fresh water, a small harbor, and access to the waters on both sides of the Keys. The island was then owned by Charles Howe of Indian Key, and the settlers leased their property from him. Populated mostly by Bahamian farmers, fishermen, and wreckers, the settlement grew steadily. One of the cash crops the settlers are known to have attempted was sugarcane. Although reports of Key Vaca's population vary widely, reasonable estimates are that there were close to 100 settlers in 1835 and near 200 in 1840. Certainly, at the time, it was the largest settlement in the Keys outside of Key West.

Joshua Appleby – Enterprising Wrecker Foiled by the Commodore

Joshua Appleby was a fifty-two-year-old wrecking captain who came to the Keys from Newport, Rhode Island. In November 1822, he and his partner, Capt. John Fiveash from Norfolk, Virginia, established a small settlement on Knight Key at the western end of Key Vacas (as it was then called) which they named "Port Monroe." Three months later, these pioneer Keys developers placed a "Notice to Mariners" in *The Floridian,* a Pensacola newspaper, and probably others, announcing that Port Monroe "has the advantages of a large and spacious harbor and the proprietors are furnished with experienced pilots, good vessels, boats and provisions of all kinds to relieve those who may be so unfortunate as to get on the Florida Reef.

"We are determined that nothing on our part (that attention and industry will ensure) will be neglected for the immediate relief of the unfortunate stranger." With greater candor they might have added, "and his money."

The notice also reported that there were then four families at Port Monroe who were growing "corn, potatoes, beans, onions, cotton, and all West India fruits" with great success. Acknowledging that the water at the settlement was not very good, they advised that there was an abundant supply of good fresh water at a distance of only five miles where large vessels could water with "facility and ease." They were referring to a large sinkhole at the eastern end of Key Vaca which had long been used as a watering place by sailing vessels in the Keys.

In fact, even in the early 1820s, the Keys presented a busy maritime scene. There were wreckers and turtlers from New Providence (Nassau), Spanish fishing vessels from Havana and, in the wintertime, American fishing smacks from New England. There was a continual stream of merchant vessels through the Straits of Florida, bound to and from Gulf and

Caribbean ports. Finally, there were the privateers who preyed on them. It was from this parade of maritime traffic that Appleby and Fiveash expected to reap handsome profits.

Of particular interest to the proprietors of Port Monroe were the privateers commissioned by newly formed South American republics such as Columbia and Venezuela in rebellion against Spain. Many of these ships were captained and manned by American seamen who had been left without employment after the end of the War of 1812. While the privateers' letters of marque and reprisal authorized them only to capture or sink Spanish vessels, some of their captains were not too fussy about nationality when they came across a fat, unarmed merchantman.

One of the privateers operating in the Straits of Florida was an armed schooner, *La Centilla*, flying the flag of Columbia, but manned largely by Americans or former Americans. In February 1823, *La Centilla* arrived off Knight Key and was piloted into an anchorage at Port Monroe by Fiveash. Her captain, Charles Hopner, conferred with Appleby about a problem he had.

Under admiralty law, privateers were required to bring or send their captured vessels back to the country which commissioned them. There, a prize court would determine whether the capture was legal before the prize could be condemned and sold. For a vessel captured in the Straits of Florida by a Columbian privateer, compliance with international law required a voyage of over 1,000 miles, with the danger of recapture along the way and a delay of months before the privateer received his share of the proceeds from sale of the prize and its cargo.

To circumvent the time-consuming and risky process required by law, Hopner proposed a shortcut which would bring almost immediate profits to himself and Appleby. Hopner would bring his prizes to Port Monroe. Appleby would inspect the cargoes and give Hopner promissory notes for their value plus his expenses and profit. Hopner would then deliberately, but gently, wreck the vessels on a nearby shoal or key. At this point, Appleby would take charge of the wrecks, offload their cargoes, and ship them to some northern port to be sold. After the sales were made, Appleby would make good on his promissory notes to Hopner. For Appleby, who was nicknamed "The Deft" by an attorney, the proposal was the answer to his dreams for Port Monroe, and he was only too happy to help Hopner.

It is not known how many prizes were disposed of by Hopner and Appleby during the spring of 1823, but their grand scheme was doomed when the imperious Commodore Porter set up the headquarters of his antipiracy squadron at Key West in April of that year.

In late May and early June, two Spanish prizes captured by *La Centilla* off the northern coast of Cuba arrived at Port Monroe followed by their captor. One was a schooner, the *Bella Dolores*, and the other was a brig, the *Rosalie*. After their cargoes had been examined and appraised by Appleby, the *Bella Dolores* was run aground on a small key to the west of Port Monroe, and the *Rosalie* was run ashore on Long Key. Appleby gave Hopner promissory notes in the amount of $3,900 for the schooner's cargo of coffee. The cargo of the brig was sold for an unknown amount to the joint account of Appleby and two other wrecking captains, James Johnson and Edward Richardson. The brig's cargo was loaded aboard Johnson's and Richardson's wreckers and eventually sold in St. Marys, Charleston, and Norfolk.

During negotiations over the value of the brig's cargo, Hopner contracted Richardson to survey the Upper Keys in order to locate and buoy a good harbor where he could hide his prizes from the prying eyes of Porter's antipiracy squadron.

While the wrecked brig was being unloaded by Johnson and Richardson, another wrecking schooner, the *Comet*, arrived on the scene and was promptly engaged to take the brig's prize crew and Appleby's share of her cargo back to Port Monroe. In payment, she was given some of the brig's rigging and sails. When the *Comet* arrived at Port Monroe, Appleby hired her to carry some of the captured cargo to Key West.

In the meantime, two Spanish citizens from Havana arrived at Key West and asked for an audience with Porter. They told him that they were the owners of the brig seized by *La Centilla* and demanded the return of their property. Porter must have already received some information about the goings-on at Port Monroe, for, in a letter to the Secretary of the Navy, he wrote, "I am under the impression that the practice of wrecking Spanish vessels on our coast by Columbian cruisers [privateers], in order to secure their cargoes, has, for a long time past, been pursued to a considerable extent, and that the establishment at Key Vacas [Port Monroe] was made with this object in view."

Porter went on to request instructions as to how to handle this somewhat delicate situation, both with respect to the privateers, which were duly commissioned vessels of a foreign power, and with respect to Appleby, who he believed was acting illegally. When the *Comet* arrived at Key West with Appleby's cargo on board, Porter ordered the vessel detained and had the cargo seized, carried ashore, and placed under guard.

Porter did not wait for the Secretary of the Navy's instructions to arrive. In his usual precipitate fashion, he dispatched a letter to Appleby warning him not to dispose of any of the cargo still in his possession and not to pay any of the promissory notes until the rightful owners of the cargo had been determined.

A short time later, Porter received the news that one of the settlers at Port Monroe had been murdered in a "most atrocious" manner by one of the Spanish fishermen from Havana who frequented the place. Once again, Porter seized the initiative and sent a guard of six marines under Second Lt. Stephen Rogers, together with a small cannon, to restore law and order at Port Monroe and to arrest Appleby for his complicity in the illegal wrecking and seizure of foreign vessels and their cargoes.

Not satisfied that he had done enough to stop the illegal activities at Port Monroe, Porter sent the topsail schooner *Grampus* to intercept *La Centilla*. Proceeding toward Key Vaca, the *Grampus* sighted *La Centilla* and two smaller vessels anchored at Looe Key. However, before the *Grampus* could beat up to their position, the three vessels escaped across the reef. Having reprovisioned the marines at Port Monroe, the *Grampus* returned to Key West, bringing with her an American seaman who had deserted from *La Centilla*.

The Secretary of the Navy's reply to Porter's request for instructions, received some weeks after the foregoing incidents, agreed that the wrecking was fraudulent and directed that the seized cargo be sent to St. Augustine for legal adjudication. In Appleby's case, however, the Secretary determined that none of his activities constituted a positive violation of then-existing U.S. laws, and directed Porter to release him from arrest.

The marines departed, and Appleby resumed his efforts to make Port

Commodore Porter, Commander of the antipiracy squadron
based at Key West (courtesy of Monroe County Public Library)

Monroe a going concern. His store sold provisions and supplies to the many wreckers from New Providence and Spanish fishermen who gathered there. They were so numerous that the collector of customs at Key West argued that a customs office should be established there, especially since those vessels were not coming to Key West to enter and clear customs.

In April 1824, Appleby extended his business enterprises by underwriting, with a partner named Snyder, the construction and operation of a store on Indian Key. The Appleby-Snyder store, under the management of Silas Fletcher, previously a settler at Port Monroe, was the beginning of the permanent settlement of Indian Key.

Appleby may have thought his problems were over when he was released from arrest and the marines sailed away, but he was far from correct. The first inkling of trouble came in a letter dated September 16, 1824, posted from on board *La Centilla* at Key West. The letter demanded to know if Appleby intended to pay off on his promissory notes to Hopner (Appleby had stopped payment as directed by Commodore Porter) and threatened to take steps if they were not. Seven months later, Appleby was under arrest again, this time imprisoned at Newport, Rhode Island, as a result of a suit brought against him by Charles Hopner.

Appleby's lawyer wrote to Porter asking for a deposition to help his defense. In the letter he argued that while both Hopner and Appleby were guilty of illegal proceedings, Appleby did not deserve to be punished because he obtained little or no gain from his portion of the cargo (Porter had seized it) and his failure to pay the promissory notes resulted from Porter's directive not to. In closing, the lawyer pleaded, "This poor, weak, misled, but, as it appears to be, not malicious man, is in close prison and, but for this defence [Porter's deposition], must remain there for Life. He certainly is the most innocent of the two culprits and I know I am doing an act of friendship to his worthy and afflicted family by giving him my professional assistance."

Appleby did not spend the rest of his life in prison, in fact, he was out on bail a week after he was arrested. The case dragged on from 1825 to 1828. In the end, the jury found that Hopner and Appleby had acted "by collusion and previous concert" to deliberately wreck the prizes but, nevertheless, ordered Appleby to pay Hopner the amount of the promissory notes plus interest, a total of $7,112.

By 1830 or earlier, Appleby was back in the Keys, living in Key West and serving as captain of the fifty-two-foot wrecking schooner *Mary Ann*. With the exclusion of the Bahamian wreckers from the Keys in 1825, Port Monroe had faded into obscurity, but Appleby still considered it his property. In an ad in the *Key West Enquirer* in December 1835, he warned all persons not to hunt or otherwise trespass on Knight Key.

Following his second wife's death in 1833, Appleby sought a less strenuous career than that of a wrecking captain. In 1837, at age sixty-seven, he secured an appointment as keeper of the Sand Key Lighthouse. In October 1846, Key West was struck by the most destructive hurricane in its recorded history. Both the lighthouse at Sand Key and the one at Key West were demolished. Swept away with Appleby were his daughter, an adopted daughter, and his grandson as well as two other persons. When an officer in the Revenue Marine whose own vessel was lost in the storm heard that the Sand Key light was gone, he said, "Poor old Captain Appleby – I knew him well: He told me the first hurricane would sweep all to destruction, and alas! his prediction is verified."

Chapter 4

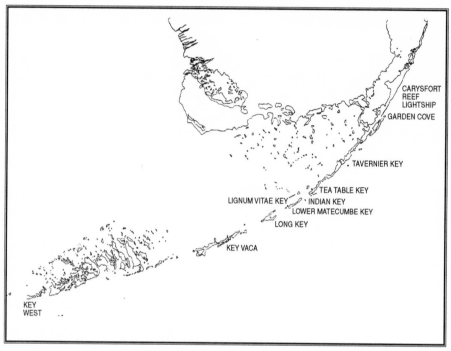

The Keys during the Second Seminole War

WAR CANOES IN THE KEYS

(1836 – 1842)

Enraged by the government's January 1836 deadline for their removal to western reservations, the Native American tribes of Florida struck back. On December 28, 1835, in central Florida, they ambushed a column of soldiers under Maj. Francis Dade, killing all but three of the 111 officers and men. On the same day, at Fort King, near present-day Ocala, Osceola killed the Seminole agent, Maj. Gen. Wiley Thompson. The Second Seminole War, the longest and bloodiest of the three Seminole wars, had begun.

In South Florida, the first blow landed at the plantation of William Cooley on New River, present-day site of Fort Lauderdale. While Cooley was away from home, a war party killed his wife, three children, and their tutor. As news of the attack spread, all the settlers on the southern mainland and those on Key Vaca fled to Key West. The *Key West Enquirer* of January 16, 1836, reported that nearly 200 refugees had arrived with nothing more than the clothes on their backs.

Only Indian Key remained occupied. With six cannons available for their defense, the residents decided to risk staying in order to safeguard their property. They threw up embankments, mounted the cannons at strategic

33

points, and formed a small militia company under Jacob Housman, a wrecking captain and leader of the island community.

Despite their distance from the mainland, the citizens of Key West were also alarmed for their safety. They dispatched a schooner to buy arms in Havana, asked the Navy to provide protection, formed a militia, and instituted nightly patrols on land and sea.

Throughout the first two years of the war, 1836 and 1837, the natives of South Florida maintained undisputed control of the mainland and made several forays into the upper Keys. Time and again, the residents of Indian Key were aroused to a state of alarm by the sight of dugout canoes moving between the neighboring keys and by the glow of campfires at night. In three separate raids, war parties burned the Cape Florida lighthouse on Key Biscayne, killing one of the keepers; attacked and burned a schooner at Tavernier Key; and ambushed and killed Captain Whalton and a crewman

Indian attack on schooner *Mary* at Tavernier Key (painting by Naya Rydzewski)

of the lightship *Florida* at Carysfort Reef as they stepped ashore on Key Largo.

The increased naval forces in the Keys by 1838 brought an end to the raids. The settlers on Indian Key relaxed their guard and disbanded the militia. The settlers who had abandoned Key Vaca returned, and the patrols at Key West were abandoned.

By 1840, naval forces in the Keys, known as the Mosquito Fleet (the antipiracy squadron of the 1820s also used this name), consisted of three schooners, five gun barges, and sixty canoes, the latter for carrying expeditions into the Everglades. The commander, Lt. John McLaughlin USN, established his headquarters on Tea Table Key about a mile east of Indian Key. Indian Key was also used as a naval depot.

At the beginning of August 1840, plans to mount a major offensive into the Everglades were set in motion. For the operation, McLaughlin withdrew all his forces from the Keys with the exception of a small detachment of five sailors under the command of a midshipman, which was left behind to care for the sick personnel on Tea Table Key.

Under the continuous pressure of expeditions into the Everglades, the natives in South Florida were running short of ammunition and food. They were well aware of the store on Indian Key, having traded there before the beginning of hostilities. A band of Spanish-speaking natives on the southwest coast known as the Spanish Indians, encouraged and advised by Spanish fishermen from Cuba, made plans to raid the island.

In the early morning hours of August 7, a war party of over 100 Spanish Indians who had been hiding on Lower Matecumbe Key silently drew up their dugout canoes on Indian Key. The chance sleeplessness of one man who awoke and saw the canoes precipitated the warriors into making a premature attack in the dark. Miraculously, of the nearly fifty inhabitants, all but ten managed to escape by hiding or getting away in boats. The next morning, the small Navy contingent from Tea Table Key launched a futile counterattack which had to be abandoned when the small cannon hastily lashed on their barges broke loose and recoiled overboard. Before the Indians left with their plunder the next afternoon, they set fires which destroyed all but two of the buildings on the Key.

After the attack on Indian Key, the native bands in South Florida were forced onto the defensive and never again moved into the Keys. Indian Key, abandoned by all but two of its families, became the Navy's major base in the Keys. McLaughlin erected barracks, storehouses, boat sheds, a hospital, and even a private residence for himself and his family.

Malarial fever was a far greater killer of soldiers and sailors than Indian bullets and arrows. The little hospital on Indian Key was continually filled with the sick and dying. In all, 45 naval personnel and one Army officer died there.

Finally, with only a few small bands of natives remaining hidden in the Everglades, the Secretary of War authorized the Florida commander to end hostilities at his discretion. By the end of May 1842, the Mosquito Fleet had passed into history and a small trickle of settlers from the Bahamas once again began to occupy the Florida Keys.

John Whalton – Lone Sentinel on the Reef

Garden Cove is a small indentation in Key Largo's eastern shoreline just north of Largo Sound. A meandering creek connects the cove with the body of water where, today, the headquarters of John Pennekamp Coral Reef State Park are located.

The cove's name dates from the 1820s, when the captain and crew of the lightship stationed at Carysfort Reef kept a small vegetable and fruit garden about a half mile up the creek. The idyllic connotation of its name belies Garden Cove's history. It was the scene of one of the tragic incidents of the Second Seminole War in the Keys.

In 1818, three years before Florida became American territory, a young man named John Whalton took up residence in St. Augustine. One year later he married a local Spanish girl. During the five years he lived there, he acquired a reputation as a public-spirited citizen as well as a skilled navigator who was well acquainted with the Florida Keys and "among the first pilots of the coast."

In 1823, Whalton was engaged by Lt. James Ramage, commanding the U.S. Schooner *Porpoise*, to serve as pilot for an expedition engaged in surveying the Florida coast. During the course of the survey, Whalton helped Ramage select potential sites for lighthouses and other aids to navigation in the Keys. In one of his reports, Ramage described Carysfort Reef as a "particularly treacherous shoal" and recommended that a floating light, as lightships were then called, be stationed there.

Congress appropriated funds for construction of a floating light for Carysfort Reef in 1824. The 220-ton, two-lantern, schooner-rigged lightship, named *Caesar*, was built in New York and completed in the spring of 1825.

In the meantime, Whalton had applied for command of a revenue cutter, but, despite a favorable endorsement from Ramage, was not selected. He next put in a bid for command of the Carysfort floating light and this time, with a glowing recommendation from the U.S. attorney for East Florida, won the appointment.

Whalton, then about twenty-five years old, arrived in Key West in July 1825 to take command of the *Caesar*. To his dismay, he learned that, on her maiden voyage from New York, the *Caesar* had been driven ashore by a storm about fifty miles north of Cape Florida. Abandoned by her contractor crew, she was salvaged by wreckers and brought to Key West. When the shipbuilder's agent arrived, he was forced to buy her back for the amount of the salvage award.

Although the *Caesar* was not seriously damaged, her stores had been lost or sold by the wreckers. It was spring of the following year before the Key West collector of customs, who was also responsible for lighthouses and lightships, was able to get her repaired, re-outfitted, and crewed.

Finding a crew proved to be the collector's most difficult job. The pay was low, the job monotonous (except when a howling gale threatened to tear the ship from her moorings), and the location isolated. The closest outposts of civilization to Carysfort Reef were the tiny settlements at Indian Key, forty miles to the southwest, and at the mouth of the Miami River, thirty miles to the north.

In April 1826, Whalton and his six crewmen anchored the *Caesar* at Carysfort Reef and lighted her two masthead lanterns, much to the disgust of the wreckers at Indian Key.

At this point, Whalton's problems were just beginning. Delivery of provisions from Key West was undependable, and prices were high. Because of this situation, the captain and his crewmen decided to plant vegetables and fruit trees in a small clearing on Key Largo. Given the low caliber of the crew and the dull routine, discipline was another problem. One man broke the ship's bell, an expensive and important aid to warning ships approaching the reef, and he was placed in irons.

Perhaps the most serious problem was that of replenishing the fresh water supply. When stocks ran low and rain failed them, they purchased water from the wreckers at fifty cents a cask, a price that strained the captain's budget. Whalton had foreseen this problem and, before taking station, had requested that his ship be provided with a thirty-foot, schooner-rigged tender to be used to obtain water from the springs near the mouth of the Miami River. Because he felt he could not trust his seamen on such extended trips, he also requested authorization to hire a mate to be in charge of the tender.

After more than a year's delay, Whalton finally got his tender and his mate, but in the meantime, he discovered that his ship was rotting away beneath him. Just six years after her launching, he sailed the *Caesar* to Key West for a survey, which revealed that she was "an entire mass of dry rot and fungus." The collector of customs added to the report of the survey, "I must say that there never was a grosser imposition practiced than by the contractor in this instance."

It probably will not surprise modern readers to learn that the same contractor who built the rotted-out *Caesar* got the contract to build another. The replacement vessel, built of rot-resistant live oak, was completed in New York in November 1830. Named the *Florida*, the 225-ton vessel was equipped to display two lights with twelve-mile visibility, a figure often disputed by passing vessels. By early 1831, Whalton and the *Florida* were anchored off Key Largo to once again warn ships away from the most treacherous section of the Florida Reef.

The monotonous life of the seven-man crew of the *Florida* was relieved by trips ashore to tend the little farm-garden and cut wood for the galley stove. When fresh water stocks ran low, the tender was dispatched with the mate in charge to sail to the mouth of the Miami River to fill the water casks.

Periodically, the captain's wife and some of his children would sail up from Key West aboard the mail boat or a wrecker to spend a few days on board. This practice was not unusual and was condoned by the Lighthouse Service as partial alleviation for the lonely nature of the duty.

In September 1835, the *Florida* was severely damaged by a gale which broke her lanterns and blew her boats away. Just three months later, as the crew was still recovering from the effects of the storm, a far more serious danger presented itself with the outbreak of Seminole hostilities. War parties moved down the coast and were seen near the mouth of the Miami River. All the settlers on the southern mainland and outlying Keys, with the exception of Indian Key, fled to Key West. Thus, in a matter of a few days, the *Florida* became the lone white man's outpost in hostile territory, and her crew lived in daily fear of attack. It is a tribute to Whalton's leadership, courage, and devotion to duty that the *Florida* remained on her station.

The campfires and dugout canoes of war parties were often seen in the upper Keys in the spring and summer of 1836. In October, a band of warriors descended on Key Largo and destroyed the lightship's farm-garden and its buildings.

Then, as months passed with no further signs of warriors in the Keys, the crew of the *Florida* began to relax their guard. Confident that the war was now confined to the mainland, Whalton allowed his wife and some of his children to sail up for a visit.

On the morning of June 23, 1837, the captain and four of his crewmen embarked in one of the ship's boats to go ashore to gather wood. Leaving his family on board in the care of the mate, the captain and his men rowed the six miles to Garden Cove. Incredible as it may seem, they were, according to one account, unarmed.

As the boat beached and the crew began stepping ashore, a volley of musket fire erupted from behind some water casks left on shore. Whalton and one of his men fell dead instantly; two other men were wounded. The three survivors shoved the boat away from the shore, jumped in, and began rowing for their lives. Six warriors emerged from behind the casks and reloaded their guns. Then, dashing into the water to shorten the range, they took aim. Fortunately, the guns, wetted by the splashing, failed to fire.

The boat returned to the *Florida* with the tragic news of the death of the captain and one of the crew. The mate then managed to attract the attention of two wrecking schooners lying nearby, and they came alongside.

Death of Captain Whalton and crewman on Key Largo (painting by David Harrison Wright, courtesy of Wrecker's Museum/Oldest House, Key West)

Despite the distinct possibility that even more warriors might be lying in wait, the wreckers volunteered to go ashore and recover the bodies.

On reaching the scene, they found that both men had been scalped, stripped naked, and stabbed in several places. In addition, the captain's finger had been cut off to get his gold ring.

That evening, the wreckers took Mrs. Whalton, her children, and the two bodies to Indian Key. The following morning, with his widow and children at graveside, the dedicated captain and his crewman were interred "as decently as circumstances would permit."

Under subsequent captains, the floating light *Florida* remained on station for another fifteen years. In 1852, she was replaced by the present-day Carysfort Reef Lighthouse, the first of the six iron screw-pile structures that light the reef today.

Jacob Housman – Lord of Indian Key

As the year 1836 began, Jacob Housman, a thirty-seven-year-old wrecking captain from Staten Island, New York, surveyed his island domain and smiled with satisfaction at the thought that he had very nearly achieved all his plans for power and wealth. In the short space of six years, he had developed the tiny eleven-acre island named Indian Key into a busy wrecking port and a tropical paradise. He held a claim to the island and owned nearly everything on it. In addition to a store, the only one in South Florida outside of Key West, he owned four wrecking vessels; a hotel; nearly thirty houses, cottages, and workshops; four wharves; a large warehouse; and a dozen or more Negro slaves. His annual income was in the tens of thousands. He lived in a large two-story mansion graced by a beautiful wife. Almost everyone on the island worked for him or was obligated to him in one way or another. Within a month's time, the territorial legislature would grant him one of his greatest desires, to make Indian Key independent of the authorities at Key West. Jacob had nearly everything he wanted or dreamed of, but, in the process of getting them, he had also acquired many enemies.

Just four days after the new year began, an incident took place which was to bring Jacob to eventual ruin. On that day, with the murder of the William Cooley family at New River, the Second Seminole War broke out in South Florida. It was the beginning of the end for Jacob Housman.

Jacob had first arrived in the Keys in the early 1820s in a small schooner he had "borrowed," without asking, from his father. He ran aground on the reef and was forced to put into Key West for repairs. While there, he quickly learned enough about the wrecking business to realize that it presented a unique opportunity to satisfy his unquenchable thirst for money and power. Knowing that he would not be welcomed home, he decided to stay in the Keys and get his share of the spoils.

At the time Jacob began to patrol the reef, the wrecking business was controlled by a few Key West merchants who owned all the wharves, warehouses, and ship repair facilities in town as well as a number of wrecking vessels. Through collusive agreements they were able to reap most of the wrecking profits for themselves. Soon, chafing under their monopoly of the business, Jacob began to look for ways to circumvent them.

41

In 1825, he came across a wrecked and abandoned French brig. He offloaded the cargo to his schooner, and, after some delay during which his movements are unknown, carried it to St. Augustine, the next nearest port of entry to Key West. The Key West merchants were enraged that he had not dealt with them, and one of them, Fielding Browne, charged him with robbery.

At St. Augustine, Jacob took advantage of a territorial law which allowed salvage claims to be decided by a five-man jury. For reasons which we can only guess, the jury awarded him an extremely generous ninety-five percent of the value of the cargo. Unfortunately for Jacob, it happened that the French consul was in town, and he appealed the jury's decision to the Superior Court there. The court declared the territorial law unconstitutional and reduced Jacob's award to two-thirds of the cargo's value.

In reply to Browne's charge of robbery, Jacob said the reason he took the cargo to St. Augustine was to avoid dealing with the dishonest Key West merchants who were "gentlemen of many avocations"; that is, they controlled all facets of the wrecking business.

The Key Westers' low opinion of Housman was reinforced by a newspaper story in 1828 that he had given a kickback to the captain of another wrecked French brig, the *Vigilant*. After being refloated, the *Vigilant* had been escorted into the harbor at Key Vacas by two wreckers. At this point, Jacob appeared on the scene and offered to pilot the brig to Key West for seventy-five percent of the value of the vessel and its cargo, which happened to include $32,000 in coin. According to the newspaper report, the French captain became a willing listener when Jacob offered to turn over part of his fee to the captain to keep for himself. The vessel and cargo were sold at Key West and, after paying off one of the original salvors with $6,000, Jacob and the Frenchman sailed for Charleston with the rest of the money.

It was natural that during the course of his search for wrecks along the reef, Jacob would anchor at Indian Key. Long before the American flag was raised at Key West, Indian Key had been a popular rendezvous for Bahamian wreckers. It had a number of advantages from a wrecker's point of view. It was located at the approximate midpoint of the reef, yet it was reasonably close, about thirty-five miles, to Carysfort Reef, where the largest number of wrecks occurred. There was sufficient depth of water over the reef opposite Indian Key for large vessels to cross into Hawk Channel, and there was a depth of nine feet close to the island. Ample fresh water was available from sinkholes on nearby Lower Matecumbe Key. Since 1824, there had been a store to provide supplies to vessels that stopped there and by 1829, there were a half dozen families living on the island, which had a reputation of being nearly mosquito-free.

The more Jacob visited Indian Key, the more he began to shape a dream of developing it into a money-making wrecking port under his personal control. By 1830, he had accumulated enough money to begin his plan. He moved to the island and bought one of the existing houses. In 1831, for $5,000, he purchased the store along with a two-story house which served as a hotel. It had a nine-pin bowling alley and a billiard table for the amusement of visiting seamen. The purchase price also included the rights to a claim of ownership of the entire island.

In that same year, Jacob's maneuvers in another wrecking incident again brought him unfavorable notice in Key West. He and another wrecker salvaged a brig and her cargo and brought them to Key West. By this time, a federal superior court had been established in Key West to settle salvage claims and issue wreckers' licenses. But instead of submitting his claim to the court, Jacob, saying he had the consent of the captain of the wrecked brig, got "two disinterested persons" to decide his claim. They rewarded him with fifty-six percent of the net value of the brig. The brig owners' agent, claiming the captain had never agreed to arbitration, sued Housman and the other wrecker in Superior Court. The judge, convinced that both sides were lying, reduced Housman's award to twenty-five percent. The Key West merchants once again loudly condemned Housman for his chicanery.

Disdainful of the uproar in Key West, Jacob pursued his plans for making Indian Key into his own tropical commercial empire. He laid out the streets and a town square in an orderly fashion. Using slave labor, he constructed wharves and a large warehouse to provide for mooring wrecking vessels and storing salvaged cargoes. He imported great quantities of fertile soil and planted coconut palms, fruit trees, and gardens. He built houses and shops for his workers, who included ships' carpenters, sailmakers, clerks, and a blacksmith.

The store was doing a booming business, not only with the wreckers, turtlers, and fishermen, but also with the natives who came in their dugout canoes from the mainland and with settlers from the Biscayne Bay area and the growing Bahamian community on Key Vaca. By the late 1800s, the store was grossing $30,000 annually.

Most of the people who dealt at the Indian Key store were poor. Jacob readily advanced them credit and then used their indebtedness as a lever to get them to perform various favors for him. One of these was to report to him news of any wrecks they might sight or hear of. It was understood that if the report resulted in Jacob getting a wreck for himself or one of his other vessels, there would be a reward. Another favor was to appear as "disinterested" witnesses in Jacob's behalf in salvage claim proceedings.

A visitor to the island in 1833 claimed that Housman's agents, upon sighting a wreck, would, instead of going to its aid or informing a nearby wrecker, sail forty or sixty miles to Indian Key to bring word to Housman. If there were other wreckers in port, Jacob would wait until nightfall when they were entertaining themselves in his hotel before getting underway for the wreck.

Jacob seemed to have an uncanny ability to persuade captains of wrecked vessels to act in his favor. In 1833, he was consorted (in partnership) with two other wreckers. One of them refloated a wrecked schooner, the *North Carolina*, and brought it to Indian Key. Jacob was not involved in the actual salvage, but, because of the consortship agreement, he was still entitled to a share of the salvage award. Without telling the captain of the wrecked schooner of this fact, he persuaded him to consign the schooner and its cargo of cotton to himself as agent. He also convinced the captain to accept arbitration of the salvage claim by two "disinterested" Indian Key residents.

In setting the award, Housman's two toadies valued the cotton, which had cost $30 a bale, at only $20 a bale. Part of the salvage award was paid off with the salvaged cotton. Jacob was able to sell part of his cotton for $50 a bale in Charleston. He was sued in Superior Court by the cotton consignee's agent. The judge ruled that the agreement between Housman and the captain was fraudulent and ordered the return of the unsold bales. Jacob appealed the decision to the Supreme Court which, many years later, upheld the lower court's ruling, saying, "the transactions at Indian Key were evidently in bad faith" and "the salvors by their conduct have forfeited all claims to compensation, even for services rendered."

Despite this setback, Jacob's fortunes continued to improve. By 1834, he was reported to have spent $40,000 on developing the island and owned four wrecking vessels. In 1832, the island's growing commerce had qualified it for an Inspector of Customs and in 1834, a post office was authorized.

About this time, Jacob built a large two-story mansion near the center of the island. Described as "elegant" by one visitor, it had a row of palm trees in front, a grove of lemon and orange trees on one side, and a garden. Behind the house along a fence were the slave quarters. Soon after its completion, Jacob returned from a voyage to Charleston with an attractive woman whom he introduced as his bride, Elizabeth Ann.

The attitude of Key Westers toward Housman is well illustrated by an entry in the diary of one of the island's lawyers. He was aboard a wrecking vessel which anchored at Indian Key for several days. He wrote, "I dislike Indian Key so much that I am determined not to go on shore unless I have some business there."

But Jacob was galled by the continuing need to deal with the Key West merchants and lawyers, who had nothing but contempt for him, and by the fact that he was subject to authorities there who he felt sided with the powerful commercial interests. After much thought, he hit upon a scheme which would greatly reduce the degree of control exercised by Key West over Indian Key. Sometime in 1835, he drew up a petition to the territorial Legislative Council requesting that Monroe County be divided into two counties. The line separating the two was to be drawn at the west end of Bahia Honda Key, and the new county was to include all the middle and upper Keys as well as a huge section of the southern mainland. The rationale for the division was that jurors from the mainland and the middle and upper Keys were required to travel great distances and be away from home many days at considerable expense when called to jury duty in Key West.

Apparently, Jacob's persuasive powers worked as well with the Legislative Council as they did with captains of wrecked ships. On February 4, 1836, the council created the new county just as requested in the petition.

Naturally, Jacob had made no attempt to inform the citizens of Key West of what he was doing, and they only learned of it after it had become fact. The *Key West Enquirer* called it "one of the wildest schemes that we have heard of lately." The merchants, lawyers, and civil authorities were enraged and petitioned to have the division rescinded, but to no avail.

Indian Key was designated as the temporary county seat. To perpetuate that choice, Jacob built a courthouse with his own money. The county officials were almost entirely his employees or associates. The first clerk of the court was Jacob's longtime chief clerk. The first county judge was his personal attorney. A carpenter who was one of the "disinterested" arbitrators of the *North Carolina* salvage claim was a justice of the peace and later sheriff. Another justice of the peace was a marble cutter from New York hired by Jacob to build a cistern. For all practical purposes, Jacob Housman now ruled not only Indian Key but all of the new county.

The Legislative Council named the new county Dade after the Major whose column of soldiers had been ambushed and massacred by the Seminoles just a month earlier. While the other settlers in South Florida and on the Keys fled their homes, those at Indian Key remained. Jacob was not about to abandon his little empire to the savages. He organized a militia company for its defense comprised of twenty-four men, at least six of whom were slaves. Expecting to be repaid by the government, he furnished them with pay, subsistence, and arms from his own resources. Not surprisingly, Jacob was elected captain. The residents threw up defensive embankments around the island and mounted six cannon at strategic points. Jacob donated one of his wrecking vessels, armed and anchored offshore, as a place of refuge for women and children in case the island should be overrun.

For the next two years, the islanders lived in more or less continual fear of attack. In March 1836, an old Spaniard arrived at Indian Key in a canoe, saying he had come to trade at the store. The islanders, knowing the natives of southwest Florida were friendly with Spanish fishermen from Cuba, suspected that he had come to spy. They grilled the old man until he admitted that he had been accompanied by two natives who were waiting for him on a nearby Key. A search party found his companions on Lignum Vitae Key, seized them, and placed them in custody together with the old Spaniard.

Two months later, the revenue cutter *Dexter* arrived to protect the island, and the prisoners were transferred on board. Incredibly, a month later, they managed to free themselves from their irons and jump overboard. One was shot and killed, but the other swam away unharmed and reached the shore of a nearby key. Upon hearing the news of the loss of his companions, the old Spaniard died.

A letter was immediately dispatched to Commodore Alexander Dallas, commander of the West India Squadron. Signed by Housman, Howe, and Fletcher, it read, "We have frequently witnessed their [the Indians'] fires between us and the Main Land and a few days Since, 4 Canoes was [sic] seen within a few miles of this Island . . . It is evident . . . that a large body of them are lurking about us and are only waiting to ascertain our situation and a favorable opportunity to make a desperate rush upon us." The letter pleaded with the commodore to order the immediate return of the *Dexter*, which was about to depart for resupply.

The *Dexter* did not return to Indian Key until July and then left again in October. In the meantime, a war party, having been informed by their spy that Indian Key was well defended with cannons, attacked an easier target: the lighthouse at Cape Florida (on Key Biscayne). Bands of warriors continued to menace the upper Keys and keep the residents of Indian Key in a state of alarm throughout the remainder of 1836 and most of the following year. In June 1837, they ambushed and killed Captain Whalton and one crewman of the lightship *Florida* as they came ashore on Key Largo.

After this last incident, Jacob and his followers sent another petition, this time to the Secretary of the Treasury, requesting that a revenue cutter be stationed permanently at Indian Key to protect them. The petition pointed out that "The peculiar Situation of Indian Key renders it liable to incursions from these hostile savages more than any other location on the coast; the temptation too is considerable inasmuch as a large store is kept on the key which is at all times filled with provissions [sic] and munitions of war for the use of the inhabitants and wreckers engaged on the coast, and these facts are well known to the Indians, they having previous to the breaking out of hostilities been in the habit of trading at this store." The petition went on to say that it had already cost the inhabitants – that is, Housman – $9,000 to protect themselves and they ought not to have to bear this expense.

Although Jacob now ruled Indian Key, he was still obliged to bring any salvaged ships and cargoes to Key West, the only nearby port of entry. If he could get Indian Key designated as a port of entry, he would be entirely free of the monopoly exercised by the Key West merchants. When an expedition of sailors and marines, on their way to hunt natives in the Everglades, stopped at Indian Key in October 1836, Jacob had an inspiration. He took his petition for a port of entry to the grog shop and offered a glass of rum to every sailor and marine who would sign it. Needless to say, he got a number of signatures; in fact, some were even willing to sign it more than once with different names. The petition was submitted to Congress but, perhaps because the subterfuge was apparent, nothing came of it.

Jacob submitted another petition for a port of entry designation in 1838. This time the powers at Key West got word of it and reacted with a strongly worded remonstrance to Congress which read in part, "The character of Jacob Housman, the proprietor of Indian Key, well known upon this coast, affords no guaranty that a privilege of a port of entry upon his island will not be abused." The petition referred to wrecking cases in which Housman had been found guilty of embezzlement of salvaged cargoes and of conspiring with the captain of a wrecked ship to defraud the owners and underwriters and continued, "Mr. Housman combines in himself, the legislative, judicial, and executive authority as lord of his insular proprietory . . . allow the entry and landing of wrecked goods at that place where there is neither a court, nor law to restrain the cupidity of the proprietor; and the undersigned submit to Congress, what security salvors, owners or underwriters can have, for their respective rights."

One more attempt for a port of entry was made in 1839, this time by Jacob's lawyer, Thomas Jefferson Smith. Smith had come to Indian Key in 1837 for his health and was the only person, other than Jacob's wife, to leave behind some complimentary remarks about him. Five years after Housman's death, Smith wrote: "[Housman] combined skill, bravery, coolness & discretion with great personal strength to a pre-eminent degree . . . a man strictly of his word, correct in his deportment and honest in his dealings." If these words are difficult to reconcile with Jacob's record, it should be remembered that Smith was Housman's "confidential and legal adviser and attorney." According to William Whitehead, Key West collector of customs, Smith's character, where best known, was such as not to entitle him to the notice of gentlemen.

In the petition, Smith argued that the dangers of moving a wrecked vessel or its salvaged cargo over the long distance to Key West and the lack of competition at Key West favored establishing a port of entry at Indian Key. The petition was supported by a number of northern insurance underwriters and merchants who were interested in creating more competition in the wrecking business. The petition was challenged by Whitehead, who charged that it contained inaccurate and distorted facts. Congress did not authorize the port of entry.

Because of the Seminole War and the consequent loss of trade at his store, Jacob's income was shrinking. Added to his financial burdens was the expense of maintaining the militia company. However, despite the danger from the hostile natives, there was still the wrecking business. Even his enemies agreed that Jacob was a man who knew no fear, and he continued to patrol the reef looking for wrecks.

Jacob's dealings in several earlier salvage incidents might be termed shady practices, but up to this point he had not been found guilty of violating any laws. In November 1836, possibly driven by his declining revenues, he stepped over the line. He and the captain of one of his wreckers were charged by the captain of the *Ajax*, a large merchantman which had wrecked on Carysfort Reef, with embezzling goods they had removed from the ship while attempting to refloat her. According to the charge, they had landed cargo at Indian Key which was "unaccounted for to this day." Judge James Webb of the Superior Court at Key West was convinced of the truth of the charge and ordered Jacob to forfeit his share of the salvage award. Perhaps because Jacob appealed the decision, the judge did not take away his license.

Neither the Seminole War, nor the loss of revenue at his store, nor the failure of Congress to honor his request for reimbursement for the cost of maintaining the militia deterred Jacob from continuing to improve his island domain. In 1837, he hired a marble cutter from New York to cut a large cistern out of the coral rock at a cost of $4,000.

As the Seminole War continued and gradually moved southward from central Florida, the naval forces in the Keys were increased. Their mission was to protect settlers and shipping in the area, to prevent arms and supplies from reaching the Seminoles from Cuba and the Bahamas, and to conduct offensive operations along the southern mainland coast and into the Everglades. By March 1838, because of the added patrols in the area, Jacob felt that the island was sufficiently well protected to disband his militia. In October, the commanding officer of the revenue cutter *Campbell* established an outpost on nearby Tea Table Key, giving the islanders a further sense of security.

While Jacob's concern with the Seminole War appeared to be fading away, his troubles with the courts were not. He had appealed the decisions against him in both the *North Carolina* and the *Ajax* cases and in both instances the Court of Appeals upheld the original court ruling. A short time later, in the fall of 1838, his career as a wrecker was ended. Judge Webb revoked his wrecker's license on a proven charge of embezzlement. Jacob, in company with his other three wrecking vessels, had removed a quantity of cargo from another large merchantman wrecked on Carysfort Reef. He failed to deliver the cargo at Key West and was reported to have stopped at Indian Key after leaving the wreck. It is difficult to imagine how Jacob thought he could get away with such a move in view of all the enemies he had in the wrecking community. It can only be surmised that he was desperate for cash. Not only did he lose his license, but he was also denied any salvage award for his four vessels.

Soon thereafter, on Christmas Day 1838, the distinguished horticulturist and physician Dr. Henry Perrine, with his family, arrived to take up temporary residence on Indian Key. Upon the cessation of hostilities, Perrine planned to move to a land grant on the southern mainland to start a settlement which would be devoted to the cultivation of commercially useful tropical plants.

With his wrecking income gone, Jacob was looking for other sources of income and became interested in the potential of tropical plants as explained to him by the enthusiastic Perrine. He also saw Perrine, with his influence in Congress, as a lever for another try for a port of entry. For his part, Perrine considered Housman the only other man in the area who had "the taste and the means to propagate and preserve precious plants."

Little is known of Jacob's agricultural ventures. He had a plantation on Lower Matecumbe, crop unknown, and another on Lignum Vitae on which he was attempting to raise coffee bean plants. Many years later, Perrine's son recalled that Lignum Vitae was "the island where Capt. Housman formerly had extensive improvements." It is also known from a letter written by Perrine that Jacob had plans in the summer of 1840 to plant on Long Key and also to start his own settlement on the southern mainland, presumably for raising tropical plants.

Charles Howe, the island's inspector of customs and postmaster, was also Perrine's partner in the Tropical Plant Co. As far as can be determined, the relationship between Jacob, on the one hand, and Howe and Perrine, on the other, was strictly business. Howe had been a resident of the island since at least 1832 and was interested in its development and improvement. But he also knew Housman well and knew he was a schemer and a man without principles.

The Bahamian settlers on Key Vaca had fled to Key West at the outbreak of the Seminole War. In the summer of 1836, they began returning to their homes. They were not happy to find themselves part of a new county under the domination of the "autocrat" of Indian Key. Nor were they happy with the administration of justice by his lackeys. In 1839, encouraged and supported by Jacob's enemies in Key West, they petitioned the Legislative Council to repeal the law that had created Dade County, or, failing that, to repeal the part of the law that established a county court and a superior court there. They complained about the "perfect irresponsibility" of the officials at Indian Key and said that as a result of the "superior power which wealth and position always gives, all power both Executive and Judicial is exercised by one man, the proprietor of Indian Key."

To substantiate the latter statement, they submitted affidavits attesting that, by Housman's order and without judicial proceedings, four seamen had been confined in stocks in his warehouse on biscuits and water for up to three days. However, in late 1839, a grand jury empaneled at Indian Key and, of necessity, composed of Jacob's supporters, acquitted him of a charge of false imprisonment.

A committee of the territorial legislature agreed that it was impossible to obtain justice in Dade County under the circumstances. They did not think it advisable to reunite the two counties, but recommended that jurisdiction in Dade County cases be transferred to Monroe County courts. A measure to that effect was introduced but was defeated by Housman's supporters in the House.

The Superior Court which met annually at Indian Key had the same judge as the Superior Court at Key West. Judge Webb, who had revoked Jacob's wrecker's license, was succeeded by Judge William Marvin in 1839. Apparently Jacob's enmity toward the court carried over to the new judge. When Walter Maloney, who was also Jacob's clerk, resigned as the clerk of the Superior Court at Indian Key in 1839, Marvin asked Housman to nominate a successor. Jacob told him that he had asked four "Respectable and competent Gentlemen," all of whom refused to accept any favor from the judge and as for himself, "You should have known that any gift of yours would be promptly refused."

Jacob did not let the matter rest there. He sent a statement to the territorial Senate complaining that Marvin's report of the grand jury's proceedings contained "very Serious slanders," was "evidently malicious," and that Marvin "has long been my most bitter and powerful enemy." The committee to whom the complaint was referred did not consider it worthy of any action.

Ever since the loss of his wrecking license in the fall of 1838, Jacob's income had gone into a steep decline. The Navy had begun using Indian Key as a storage depot, and his store did some business with the naval forces, but not nearly enough to offset the income from wrecking. By March 1840, his finances had sunk so low that he was forced to mortgage the island and the buildings he owned to two Charleston men for $16,000.

Jacob was now desperately searching for any means to recoup his fortunes. It was the Indians, he told himself, who were responsible for much of his loss of income, so why not turn the tables and make them the means of recouping his finances? He sent a proposal to the governor and Legislative Council of Florida and the president and Congress of the United States. In it he offered to "catch or kill all the Indians of South Florida for two hundred dollars each." How Jacob proposed to do this was not explained, but, given his personal courage and strength and his drive when it came to making money, there is no doubt that he would have made a very determined attempt.

Members of Florida's House of Representatives actually took the proposal seriously and voted to recommend favorable consideration to the president. The Florida Senate did not agree, and Congress was not interested either.

The land in South Florida on which Perrine planned to start his tropical-plant agricultural settlement had been granted to him by an act of Congress for his services to the government. With his usual nerve, Jacob reasoned: if Perrine, why not me? He addressed a petition to Congress asking that he, too, be granted land in South Florida to start a settlement. There is a hint in the petition that Jacob was beginning to lose touch with reality. Not only did he ask Congress to grant him the land, for which he had done nothing, but he also asked the government to grant all the settlers living within a radius of three miles of the center of the grant the "rights of self government" and freedom from "all control of all officers and all laws of the revenue, naval, and military department of the Government of the United States." Needless to say, his preposterous petition received no consideration.

At the beginning of 1840, the further-strengthened naval forces in the Keys, now known as the "Mosquito Fleet," were under the command of Lieutenant McLaughlin. He continued to use Indian Key as a storage depot until the spring, when he established his headquarters, including storage facilities and a small hospital, on Tea Table Key, about a mile away from Indian Key. The reason for the move has never been determined, but possibly, Jacob was making unreasonable demands for rental of his storage facilities.

McLaughlin's primary mission was to track down and capture or kill the natives hiding in the Everglades. For this purpose he had a large number of canoes and conducted intensive exercises on Tea Table Key to train sailors in the handling of canoes and the use of small arms.

At the beginning of August, everything was in readiness for a major offensive into the Everglades. All the able-bodied men at Tea Table Key were sent on the expedition except five who, under the command of Passed Midshipman Murray, were left behind to care for the sick.

It was beyond any military officer's wildest imagination that the native warriors on the mainland would travel over thirty miles of water to launch an attack on Indian Key. But, at the very moment the expedition left Tea

Sailors and marines of the Mosquito Fleet in the Everglades
(courtesy of National Archives)

Table Key, they were being watched by a large war party lying in concealment on Lower Matecumbe Key. Over 100 in number, these natives of the southwest coast, under their giant leader, Chief Chakaika, were known as the Spanish Indians. According to Chakaika's sister, who was later captured, three Spaniards had visited their camp in the Everglades and supplied them with detailed information about Indian Key and advice on how to attack it.

When Chakaika saw the ships sail away, he knew the moment had arrived to launch his attack. At about 2 A.M. on the morning of August 7, seventeen dugout canoes beached on the southwestern shore of Indian Key. The warriors moved silently ashore and took up places of concealment waiting for first light to begin their attack. Shortly thereafter, a carpenter, James Glass, unable to sleep, looked out his door and saw the canoes. He awoke his neighbor and the two men headed for Housman's house, where they knew there was a store of arms and ammunition. On the way, they stumbled across the war party, shots were exchanged, and the Spanish Indians began their attack.

Upon hearing the shots and war cries, Jacob and Elizabeth Ann ran downstairs to get the guns, which were kept near the front door. Just as they reached the bottom of the stairs, the Indians burst through the front door. The Housmans turned and ran out the back door and down to the shore. They waded out as far as they could and then, slipping off their night-clothes, began swimming toward the outer end of the two L-shaped wharves. As they started off, they were overtaken by two of their dogs, both of them barking loudly. Unable to silence them by command, Jacob was forced to drown each of them in turn. When they reached the end of one of the wharves, Jacob left Elizabeth Ann clinging to a piling while he swam around to where his boats were tied up.

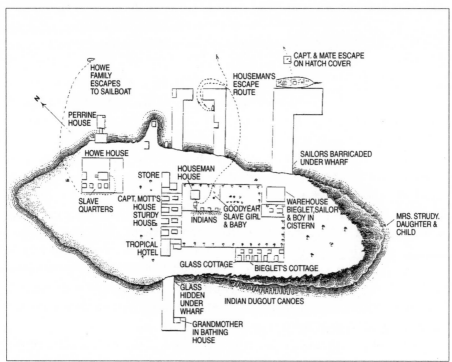

Indian Key August 7, 1840, showing escape routes of some inhabitants
(based on a drawing by Henry E. Perrine in *A True Story of Some Eventful Years in Grandpa's Life*)

55

Biding his time until none of the Indians were near the shore, Jacob managed to untie one of his boats and push it around to where Elizabeth Ann was waiting. The two climbed in and rowed to a schooner anchored near Tea Table Key. They reported the situation to Murray and then watched in despair as the tiny naval force in two barges made a futile counterattack.

The next day, Jacob and the other survivors on the schooner saw the Indians going from building to building setting each on fire. Soon, the whole island was a mass of flames and smoke. Standing there, watching his island domain being reduced to a pile of ashes, Jacob, outwardly calm and puffing a cigar, remarked, "Well, there goes two hundred thousand dollars."

McLaughlin returned to Indian Key as soon as he received word of the attack. He conferred with Jacob, who agreed to turn the island over to the Navy for use as a base until the end of hostilities. In October, Jacob and Elizabeth Ann left Indian Key, never to return. In a letter, Howe reported that Housman had "cleared out for good – took everything he had left, to Key West, . . . to sell at Auction – his Negros – Boats – vessels & I think I see his object, he is as usual very schemy [sic], he is a good deal in debt & it was thought before the invasion, that he could not stand it more than a year or two longer . . . I could not but feel sorry for the man, notwithstanding his unprincipled disposition."

In Key West, Jacob found work as a seaman aboard a wrecker. Nine months after the Spanish Indians destroyed his little empire, Jacob was killed when, in a heavy sea, he was crushed between his vessel and the hull of a wreck. Elizabeth Ann buried him on Indian Key beneath a marble tombstone with this somewhat-less-than-candid inscription:

"Here lieth the body of Captain Jacob Housman, proprietor of this island who died by accident May 1, 1841, aged 44 years and 11 months. To his friends he was sincere, to his enemies he was kind, to all men faithful. This monument is erected by his most disconsolate though affectionate wife, Elizabeth Ann Housman. Sic Transit Gloria Mundi."

Housman lived his life in the pioneer days of the Florida Keys to the fullest. He was bold, brave, strong, and determined. He seized every opportunity to turn circumstances and events to his advantage, sometimes with complete disregard for the law or moral principles. He probably felt justified in doing so, considering the hold on the wrecking business exercised by the powerful merchants of Key West and their allies, the lawyers and the judges. He was not the only wrecking captain to yield to temptation, but, as the best known, he did much harm to the public's image of the wrecking business.

Perrine Family – High Hopes Meet a Tragic End

On Christmas Day, 1838, a brig dropped anchor off Indian Key. On board was the horticulturist and physician Henry Perrine. The doctor was accompanied by his wife, Ann; two teenage daughters, Sarah and Hester; and a son, Henry E., age eleven. The family was welcomed by Charles Howe, postmaster and inspector of customs at Indian Key and also Perrine's business partner.

While serving as a U.S. consul in Mexico, Perrine had become interested in the cultivation of tropical plants and had conceived a plan for a settlement in South Florida to be devoted to raising commercially useful tropical plants. Among those he expected to grow were agave (sisal), used for making rope; logwood and cochineal cactus, used for making dyes; mulberry, used to feed silkworms; cotton, and others. During a visit to the Keys in 1837, he had discussed his plans with Judge Webb of the Superior Court in Key West and Howe, and they became his partners in the Tropical Plant Company.

Just six months before arriving at Indian Key, Perrine had received the welcome news that, for his services to the government, Congress had passed an act granting him a township (six-mile square) in South Florida in which to establish his tropical-plant agricultural settlement. Because the Seminole War prevented him from occupying the grant, he decided to settle temporarily on Indian Key, where Howe was already successfully cultivating some of the plants the doctor had sent him.

Much later in their lives, Perrine's son Henry and his daughter Hester wrote their recollections of their experiences on Indian Key. Most of the story that follows is taken from those memoirs. Henry's memory of Indian Key as it looked on the day of their arrival is perhaps the best description of the island that we have.

We saw on the distant horizon the top of palm trees which appeared at first as though floating in the air . . . Soon the tops of houses could be seen, and then the whole island of Indian Key in all its then beauty greeted our eager eyes. That little island of only twelve acres was to be our home until the war with the Seminole Indians should cease . . . A large warehouse three stories in height, and crowned with a lofty cupola, was the most prominent object. A short distance beyond, stood the two-story mansion of Captain Houseman, the proprietor of nearly all the island and of the various cottages, shops, stores, hotel and warehouse. There were about forty buildings in all, none of them of pretentious architecture, but nearly all having either the graceful palm trees, or others of a tropical or semi-tropical nature near their doors. Three large wharves stretched out from the northeastern side of the island; beyond these was a small neck of land, upon which stood a carpenter's shop and a blacksmith shop. About a hundred feet beyond, stood a two-and-a-half-story house with a cupola upon it, and having both upper and lower verandas on the side facing the sea and the small wharf in front . . . Right opposite this house, which was to be our home, stood the low one-story house and negro dwellings belonging to Mr. Charles Howe . . . On the southwestern side of the island, another long wharf stretched out to deep water. The side of the island towards the gulf consisted of jagged coral rock, while on the opposite side was a sandy beach.

Most of the island's residents were wreckers and turtlers. Others were storekeepers, carpenters, blacksmiths, laborers, and slaves. Nearly all of them owed their allegiance to Jacob Housman either as his employees, slaves, or through indebtedness to him. The Perrines had very little in common with these people, and, as a result, their social life was very circumscribed. The only family they considered socially acceptable was that of Howe. The Howes had five children, all of them younger than the Perrine children, and seven slaves. Housman was also married and owned slaves, but was not welcomed into the Perrine family circle because his wife was considered to be a woman of "bad reputation."

When the naval officers of the "Mosquito Fleet" heard of the presence of two young ladies on Indian Key, they dubbed them the "belles of the reef" and came to call. Perrine would not allow them to meet his daughters, saying they were only schoolgirls and were busy at their studies. Despite this rebuff, the officers would sometimes come in their boats after dark to serenade the "belles" and, in the process, make the doctor very angry.

Perrine established a nursery for experimenting with various tropical plants on nearby Lower Matecumbe Key. He also visited the Bahamian settlers on Key Vaca from time to time both to attend to their ills and to interest them in growing tropical plants. He hoped to persuade them to resettle to his township grant on the mainland when the Seminoles were subdued.

On one occasion when Perrine was summoned to Key Vaca to treat a seriously ill settler, he decided to take his daughter Hester with him. Here are Hester's recollections of the trip:

> We embarked on a small 'fishing smack,' sloop rigged, and only a very small cabin; not large enough to stand upright in, as it was not intended for night service. After a few miles had been sailed, a severe storm came up and we were obliged to come to anchor to leeward of one of the islands. There was only room to put me down in the cabin and batten the hatch down, while poor Father sat wrapped in a waterproof on the bow of the boat drenched by the waves that swept over the deck, and I the most seasick mortal that you can imagine!
>
> But the storm soon blew over, and I emerged from the darkness and discomfort into the most glorious sunlight, and just at dark our voyage was completed, and we landed at 'Key Vacas.' We remained there for ten days, enjoying every moment. The simple Bahamians made a little queen of me. The sailors' wives allowing me to go to the bottom of their chests, overhauling the many curious and some valuable things that [they] had so long been gathering from the various wrecks, and giving me various little treasures.
>
> After our return, whenever a fishing smack came up from Key Vacas, there were always some gifts brought by the sailors consigned for me. Sometimes sugar cane or watermelons, or sweet potatoes and once a great 'Sweet Potato Pone' that had been baked in a great Bake Kettle. The kind hearts of these people so often wishing to give pleasures.

In the beginning, Perrine was somewhat frustrated in his efforts to get the Key Vaca Bahamians to try growing tropical plants. In 1839, they failed to plant any of the seeds he had given them, preferring instead to concentrate their efforts on edible vegetables such as sweet potato, squash, and melon. But he did manage to persuade three of the leading residents to plant Sea Island cotton and mulberry plants.

By the summer of 1840, Perrine felt that he had finally convinced the Key Vaca settlers that the production of raw silk and cotton could "easily be accomplished by the feeblest hands of their women and children alone; and that these two precious staples will afford ample funds for schools and churches." He fully expected that they would have grown a sufficient stock of plants to be ready to transplant them to his township grant on the mainland that fall or winter. As to the Seminole menace, he had a simple solution: "Give us arms and ammunition, withdraw all U.S. troops from South Florida and the actual residents of Key Vacas and Indian Key will suffice to protect the settlements of small cultivation."

To the doctor's son Henry, Indian Key was a young boy's paradise. Howe's slaves taught him how to fish and took him along on fishing trips. He learned how to swim. His father gave him a shotgun which he used to shoot birds and, once, a stray cat. For pets he had a tame cormorant and a crane, and he also had two playmates, Charles and Edward Howe, aged eight and nine. The three boys were often taken on sailing expeditions by their fathers aboard Howe's small schooner, the *Charles and Edward*.

On one memorable cruise aboard the little schooner in April 1840, they sailed north across Florida Bay and anchored by Sand Key (Sandy Key today), a few miles from Cape Sable. The next morning, they went ashore at the East Cape near the remains of an abandoned earthwork fort, a former Army outpost in the war against the Seminoles. Perrine was considering this area as a possible site for his tropical-plant settlement. With a Colt rifle in hand, the doctor scouted the area around the fort. Having found no signs of Indians, he then, as was his usual custom, stopped to plant some seeds.

The expedition continued north along the Everglades' west coast, searching for a likely spot to gather oysters. Along the way, they stopped briefly at the Middle and Northwest Capes while Perrine planted more seeds. They finally anchored near the mouth of a small stream lined with mangrove trees, possibly the mouth of the Little Shark River.

The falling tide revealed a large bank thick with oysters. The schooner was moored alongside the bank, and two timbers were placed under the hull to prevent damage from the oyster shells at low tide. For two or three days, the party gathered oysters, roasted them over a fire on the bank, feasted on them, and stored the rest to take back to Indian Key.

At night they saw the light of an Indian campfire on the next point of land to the north. Incredibly, they turned in without posting a watch. Despite the captain's assurances that they had nothing to fear from the Indians, Henry lay awake listening for sounds from the mangrove forest.

On one occasion, Perrine and his son went ashore. While young Henry stood guard with a rifle, his father went from point to point planting tropical seeds. Henry was greatly relieved when his father finished and they returned to the relative safety of the schooner.

On the way home, because they were out of fresh water, they anchored at Cape Sable again. Several of the men went ashore and, by digging a hole only a few feet deep in the sandy soil, were able to fill their casks with "delicious water such as we never had at Indian Key." Favored by a fresh breeze, the *Charles and Edward* reached home that night.

In later years, Henry often thought what easy prey they would have been had they been discovered by the Indians. He was right. The Cape Sable area was known as the "Indian Hunting Grounds" because the Indians were accustomed to come there to hunt deer and catch fish in Florida Bay. Unbeknownst to Perrine and Howe, just two weeks before their visit, a detachment of sailors and marines had gone ashore at Cape Sable and had been attacked by a party of over fifty Indians. Only the fortuitous arrival of two more Navy schooners saved them from annihilation.

In order to clearly understand what happened to the Perrine family on the fateful day Chakaika and his band of Spanish Indians descended on the tiny island, it is necessary to be aware of the layout of their home. Their two-and-a-half story house was built out over the water on a stone foundation. The completely enclosed space under the house could be entered through a trapdoor in a small room on the first floor. The Perrines used the space to bathe in the salt water.

Perrine family's house on Indian Key (drawing by Henry E. Perrine in *A True Story of Some Eventful Years in Grandpa's Life*, courtesy of Monroe County Public Library)

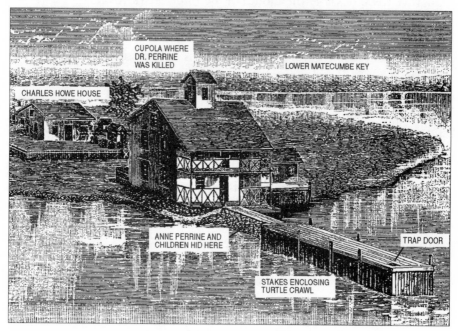

On the seaward side of the house was a long wharf connected to the house by a planked walkway over a stone foundation. Externally it appeared to be a solid stone structure but, in fact, there was an interior passageway about five feet wide and four feet high leading from the bathing area to the space under the wharf. In the early days of the Seminole War, a small escape boat had been kept hidden in the passageway. When the fear of Indian attack had been dispelled by the presence of naval forces in the area, the wharf had been completely enclosed by wood stakes to form a turtle crawl (pen) under the wharf. The stakes were closely spaced, driven into the bottom, and spiked to the wharf at their upper ends.

In addition to the small room with the trapdoor, the first floor contained a parlor and a dining room. On the second floor were four bedrooms. In the half-story above were two rooms, one used as a library, the other as a schoolroom where Sarah Perrine held classes for the Howe children. At the top of the house was a cupola which was entered by way of a steep stairway and a trapdoor.

About two o'clock in the morning of August 7, 1840, the Perrines were awakened by the sound of gunshots and savage yells. As the sounds of the attackers drew near, Perrine ordered his wife and children to hide beneath the house. After they had descended, he pulled a chest of seeds over the trapdoor.

Ann Perrine and her children crawled into the narrow passageway leading to the turtle crawl and sat down in the water at the far end. Although the tide was high, there was still about a foot of space in which to breathe.

While they sat there in their nightclothes shivering with fear and cold, the family heard the voices of the Indians as they approached the house and surrounded it. Then they heard the voice of Perrine speaking in Spanish. He told the Indians he was a physician, hoping they would assume he was a Spaniard, not an American, and leave him alone.

The Indians left, but, after a short while, returned and broke into the house. The children and their mother listened to the sounds of breaking glass and then heard a voice saying in English,[1] "they are all hid; the old man upstairs." A few minutes later, the sound of heavy blows from the top of the house indicated that the Indians were breaking through the trapdoor to the cupola. This was followed by a chorus of blood-chilling yells which they feared signaled the death of husband and father.

The remaining hours of the night passed with agonizing slowness while the mother and her three children prayed for daylight in hopes that the Indians would then depart. Shortly after daybreak, the sound of cannon reports from seaward made them believe their prayers were answered and that help was on its way. After an answering volley of musket and cannon fire from the island, there was silence, and their spirits sank once more. What they had heard were the sounds of a futile counterattack by two barges manned by sailors from the Navy hospital on Tea Table Key. When their hastily mounted cannon recoiled overboard, they were forced to retreat.

---

[1] This was probably the voice of one of the several Negroes seen among the attackers. Escaped slaves living among the Seminoles were their allies in the war.

Unable to know what the Indians were doing and not daring to leave their place of concealment, mother, daughters, and son sat and waited as the hours dragged slowly by. Then a new horror presented itself. Heavy smoke began rolling into the passageway, and they realized that their house had been set on fire. By now, the tide had fallen and they were sitting in only a few inches of water. To keep from suffocating, they held their faces near the surface of the water and splashed water over themselves or breathed through wet folds of their nightclothes. After a while, the wooden planks above them caught fire and tongues of flame darted down. In a futile attempt to contain the fire, they plastered the underside of the planks with mud from the sea bottom.

Mother and children were totally trapped, their only avenue of escape barred by the stakes enclosing the turtle crawl. As the roar of the flames consuming the house grew louder, young Henry, who had just turned thirteen, began to scream. His mother and sisters held him tightly and tried to quiet him, warning him that the Indians would hear him. But Henry tore himself away and saying he would rather be killed by the Indians than roasted alive, managed to squeeze through the stakes into the turtle crawl. Knowing his mother and sisters could not follow him, he never expected to see them alive again.

From within the crawl, Henry peered through the stakes looking for the Indians but saw none. All was quiet on the island save for the roar of the fire. Looking over toward Lower Matecumbe, he could see many canoes and some boats which belonged to the settlers drawn up on the shore. Assuming the Indians had left the island, he opened a trapdoor at the end of the wharf and climbed out. Looking back at their house, he saw that it was nearly consumed and said a silent goodbye to his mother and sisters.

When another careful survey of the island still showed no signs of life, Henry waded ashore and, walking past the open door of the store, made his way to the Housman house. He was about to go in, but, seeing the broken windows and furnishings thrown out on the ground, it occurred to him that he might find dead bodies inside. He began retracing his steps and then decided to walk out to the bathing house on the middle wharf. As he started out, he glanced over in the direction of the burning house and was overjoyed to see his mother and sisters emerging from the trapdoor at the end of the wharf. Hurrying to meet them, he noticed a large boat drawn up on

Ann Perrine, Doctor Perrine's wife (courtesy of Historical Association of Southern Florida)

the shore in front of the store, partly loaded with goods from the store.

Henry fortunately did not know that both times he passed the store, there were six Indians inside busily engaged in selecting more plunder to load in the boat. Several of the island's residents who lay in hiding nearby watched him come and go, certain the Indians would emerge and kill him at any moment.

When he reached his mother and sisters, Henry told them about the boat. The reunited group waded around the end of the point of land on which the blacksmith's shop stood and reached the boat. Sarah was so weak that they had to lift her up and roll her over the gunwale. With strength born of sheer desperation, Henry, Hester, and their mother managed to push the boat off the beach and pull it along to the end of the wharf. The boat had only one oar and one paddle. With Henry rowing and Hester paddling, they slowly drew away from the island and headed toward a schooner anchored by Tea Table Key.

Partway to safety, they saw a canoe with two Indians leave Matecumbe and head in their direction. Henry and Hester redoubled their efforts to reach safety. Sailors on the schooner sighted their boat and headed toward them in a whaleboat. The Indians, realizing they could not intercept the boat before the schooner's boat reached it, changed course for Indian Key. A little while later, the whaleboat crew took the Perrines aboard and brought them to the schooner. As they came aboard, they were met by the Howes, the Housmans, and several others who had escaped from the island, but their lingering hopes were dashed when they saw that Dr. Perrine was not among them.

Whether at this time or later, Henry's mother told him how they had escaped their fiery tomb. After Henry left, they listened for the sounds of shots or yells which would tell them that he had been discovered by the Indians and killed. Hearing nothing but the roar of the approaching flames, they began to claw away at the coarse rocks, coral, and mud at the base of one of the stakes with their bare hands. Heedless of the torn flesh and the pain, they finally succeeded in loosening the stake enough to be able to pull it to one side and squeeze through. The lifelong scars on Sarah's shoulders, made by live embers falling from the wharf, attested to the narrowness of their escape.

Mother and children watched from the deck of the schooner as their island home became a mass of flames. When the Indians finally left Lower Matecumbe and headed out across Florida Bay, a boat from the schooner proceeded to Indian Key to search for survivors. It returned with a number of settlers who had escaped by hiding in cisterns, under wharves, in bushes, and in other places, but Perrine was not among them. A few charred bones were found in the ruins of the Perrine house. They were buried on Lower Matecumbe Key beside one of the doctor's prized sisal plants. Some of those plants can still be seen today growing on Indian Key, the only visible reminder of man with a dream and his tragic end.

Chapter 5

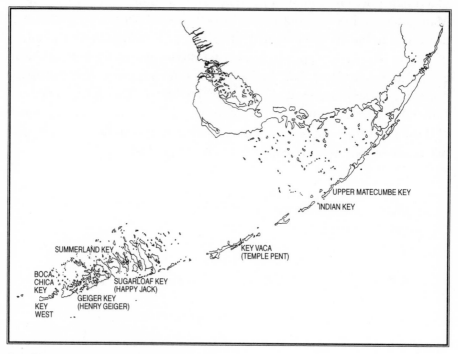

UPPER MATECUMBE KEY

INDIAN KEY

SUMMERLAND KEY

KEY VACA
(TEMPLE PENT)

BOCA
CHICA
KEY

SUGARLOAF KEY
(HAPPY JACK)

GEIGER KEY
(HENRY GEIGER)

KEY
WEST

Pre–Civil War settlements and settlers

THE VANISHED SETTLEMENTS

(1843 – 1864)

*A*fter the raid on Indian Key in 1840, the rural Keys were very nearly deserted. Most of the almost 200 settlers on Key Vaca fled to Key West. Only two families returned to Indian Key, but left when the naval forces were withdrawn at the end of the Second Seminole War in mid-1842.

At the end of the war, only a few hundred Native Americans remained in Florida, most of them hidden deep in the Everglades. Those who had not died or been killed during the war had been transported to reservations in the west. As fear of Indian attack faded, a trickle of settlers began to occupy the outlying Keys. In 1843, there were two families on Big Pine Key, a single man on Geiger Key, and seven families had applied for permits under the Armed Occupation Act to settle on the western end of Key Largo.

The first census to include all the Keys outside of Key West was taken in 1850. In the lower Keys, the census taker found thirty-two settlers scattered between Boca Chica, Sugarloaf, and Summerland Keys. In the middle Keys he found approximately forty settlers living on Key Vaca. According to a U.S. Coast surveyor, their settlement consisted of "nearly 20 houses in a line on the beach, seven miles from the west end [of Key Vaca]." In the upper Keys, Indian Key had been reoccupied by a few families who had

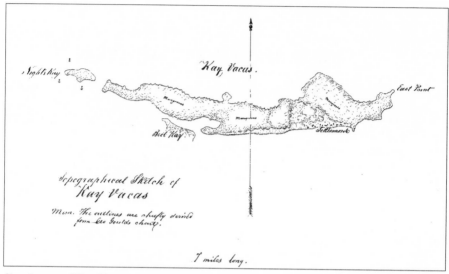

Sketch map of Key Vacas in 1849 showing settlement at Eastern End
(F. H. Gerdes, U.S. Coast Survey, courtesy of National Archives)

constructed a half dozen buildings and a wharf, but only one of the seven families that had applied to settle on Key Largo in 1843 remained in the area.

Between 1850 and 1860, there was a large turnover and gradual decline in the population of the lower and middle Keys as pioneer families, one by one, gave up the fight against the heat, the mosquitoes, the shortage of fresh water, and the isolation. At the end of the ten-year period, the combined population of the lower and middle Keys was fifty-two. Only two of the original lower Keys households remained, and settlements on three of the lower Keys had been abandoned. The settlement on Key Vaca remained, but had lost all but one of its 1850 families.

In the upper Keys in 1860 there were two families on Indian Key and three on Upper Matecumbe with a combined population of twenty seven. A reported small settlement on Key Largo in 1855 had been abandoned by 1860.

The exodus from the rural Keys continued during the Civil War (1861–1865). Out of twenty-two pioneer households there at the start of the war, only nine remained at its end, and a third of these were single men.

Approximately half of the pre–Civil War settlers were from the Bahamas. Except for a handful of other foreigners, the rest were Americans. After the raid on Indian Key, there were no more slaves in the rural Keys that we know of, and only a few free blacks, all living in the lower Keys. Very few of these settlers were literate. In 1850, out of seventeen persons over the age of twenty in the lower Keys, only seven could read and write.

The early settlers of the rural Keys lived in the most primitive conditions. Many of their houses were nothing more than thatched palmetto huts. Others were made of driftwood with thatched roofs. One of the biggest problems the pioneers faced was the scarcity of fresh water. A prime factor in the selection of a site for a settlement was the presence of a nearby sinkhole with a sufficiently large supply of water, but in extended dry periods the water would turn brackish. The only other source of fresh water was rainwater runoff from roofs, which was stored in barrels or cisterns.

The overwhelming majority of the adult males were mariners occupied in fishing, turtling, sponging, and wrecking. A few were farmers growing vegetables and fruits for the Key West market. After clearing the jungle of trees, vines, and dense underbrush, they planted melons, squash, sweet potatoes, and various fruits such as bananas, sapodillas, and limes.

Beachcombing for flotsam from ships wrecked on the reef provided valuable additions to the pioneers' meager store of materials and possessions. Washed-up lumber was used to build houses and, along with remains of rigging and sails, to construct or repair boats. The women often found clothing, dishes, and utensils. Cargo such as bales of cotton could be taken to Key West and sold for cash.

The settlers' only contacts with the outside world came when they sailed their small boats to Key West or when the occasional fisherman or wrecker would anchor nearby. Weeks, even months, could pass without any news or mail. Depending on the wind and weather, it might take anywhere from a day to a week or more to sail to Key West. If a settler became seriously ill or gravely injured, he or she might well die before reaching a doctor in Key West.

Of the approximately 150 persons who tried to make a home in the Keys wilderness between the end of the Second Seminole War and the end of the Civil War, a period of twenty-three years, only a handful were able to endure the hardships and make a living for themselves and their families. What little we know of these rugged Keys pioneers comes mainly from government records such as census reports. In rare instances, other information comes to light from diaries, letters, or newspaper and magazine stories. From these fragmented bits, the following stories of three pre–Civil War Keys pioneers have been pieced together.

Henry Geiger – The Lower Keys' First Entrepreneur

Henry Geiger was one of the first known pioneers to have settled in the lower Keys outside of Key West. In 1843, he applied for permission to establish a settlement on 160 acres of land on the east end of "Boco Chico" under the provisions of the Armed Occupation Act of 1842. The purpose of the Act was to encourage "the armed occupation and settlement of the unsettled part of the peninsula of East Florida." A person granted land under the Act had to erect a house, clear and enclose at least five acres, and reside there for five years. At such time as the land was surveyed by the government (which did not happen until 1873), the settler could apply for a patent to his property. The area on which Henry settled is a neck of land at the eastern end of Boca Chica separated from the rest of the island by a stream then called Pilot's Creek. During Henry's lifetime, the land came to be called Geiger's Key and that name remains today.

Henry was a thirty-seven-year-old bachelor when he settled on his land grant. Assisted by Robert Allen, a fifty-six-year-old free black who lived with him, he cleared the land to start a plantation. Two other single men, who lived in the vicinity and were listed as laborers, probably also worked for Henry. By 1850, the value of his personal property was recorded as $1,500, a fair sum for those days.

The diary of an unknown Boston artist contains the record of a brief visit to Henry's plantation in February 1851. With a Key West native as his guide, the artist set sail from Key West to see more of the Keys and to hunt birds. When the two men arrived at the plantation in the late afternoon, Henry was not there, but his "old Negro Bob" was. After searching in vain for something to shoot at, the visitors returned to the house and dined on a supper of fried pork and cold sweet potatoes. The artist spent the night on an old cot "with a stool to keep my legs from going through." Before leav-

Henry Geiger's home on Geiger Key in 1851 (from *Diary of Unknown Boston Artist*, courtesy of The Winterthur Library: Joseph Downs Collection of Manuscripts and Printed Ephemera)

ing the next morning, he made a pencil sketch of Geiger's home. The sketch shows a frame house with a gable roof, a chimney for a fireplace, and several outbuildings. A tall pole on the beach in front of the house may have been used to signal passing vessels. Certainly, compared with a typical Keys settler's house of those times, Henry's was luxurious.

At first, Henry grew vegetables and fruits for the Key West market, only a few hours' sail away. Then he added stove firewood to his list of products. An 1853 entry in a Key West attorney's diary reads: "This forenoon, H. Geiger brot me a cord of wood for which I paid him $3.50 and will have to pay 50 cents more to have it hauled [from the dock] up to my home. We burn about a cord of wood per month — at $4 per cord it is no small item on the year's expense." With a population of more than 2,000 in Key West to sell to, Henry's firewood business was undoubtedly clearing a tidy profit.

By 1860, Henry had added a third business pursuit. In the census for that year he listed himself as a tanner. He was probably tanning Key deer hides, using tannic acid made from the bark of red mangrove trees.

Henry lived on Geiger Key for more than twenty-seven years, but never married. After Allen died or left, sometime in the 1860s, Henry hired a mulatto woman, Affa Morris, to look after his personal needs. We do not know when Henry died, but his name disappears from the census in 1870. Henry Geiger was one of the very few pre–Civil War Keys pioneers who not only persevered in the mosquito-infested wilderness, but, with his varied pursuits, managed to make a success of it.

Temple Pent – The Squire of Key Vacas

One of the most respected pioneers of the rural Keys in pre-Civil War days was Capt. Temple Pent Sr., who, because of his prestige and influence, came to be known as Squire Pent. Self-educated, a skilled seaman and pilot, he was elected to four successive terms in the territorial legislature by his fellow settlers.

Born in the Bahamas in 1794, Temple went to sea at an early age. Serving aboard Bahamian wrecking and turtling vessels, he soon became familiar with the waters of South Florida and the Keys. He was particularly attracted to the land around the Miami River, a frequent watering stop for the Bahamian vessels. In 1810, when Florida was still Spanish territory and Temple was only sixteen, he began to clear and cultivate a tract of land in the area today known as Coconut Grove. Over the next few years he married and began to raise a family in Nassau while continuing to visit and improve his future home site on the Florida mainland. In 1821, after Florida was ceded to the United States, he became a U.S. citizen, and in 1825 moved his wife and four children to their new home in the Miami River wilderness. When the family arrived, their only neighbors were a half dozen other settlers and Seminoles, some of whom worked on the settlers' farms.

Pent's reputation as a skilled pilot came to the notice of Commodore Porter when Porter arrived in Key West in 1823 to establish a base for his antipiracy squadron. He engaged Pent to serve as the squadron's official pilot for local waters. When not engaged in piloting, Temple salvaged wrecks and carried coastal cargo as captain of the pilot schooner *Mary Elizabeth*. In 1830, he was appointed a branch pilot for Monroe County, which then included all the mainland coastal waters as far north as Lake Okeechobee.

As government pressure to remove the Seminoles from Florida to a western reservation mounted, the Seminoles became increasingly hostile.

Concerned for the safety of his large family, which in 1833 included eight children, he decided to move to Key Vacas (as Key Vaca was then called), where there was a growing community of Bahamian farmers and fishermen.

When news of the murder of a settler's family on the mainland and movement of Seminole war parties down the coast reached Key Vacas on January 15, 1836, the settlers there fled to Key West. A month later, they received more disturbing news. At the instigation of Jacob Housman, a less-than-honorable wrecking captain and the "lord" of Indian Key, Monroe County had been divided into two counties, with the new county, Dade, beginning at Bahia Honda. Pent and the rest of the Key Vaca settlers were enraged. They had not been consulted and now found themselves under the domination of a new set of county officials, all of them lackeys of Housman. Pent was one of the signers of a petition to rescind the division, but it was to no avail.

As months passed and there was no indication of Indian activity in the middle and lower Keys, the settlers began returning to Key Vacas. With his appointment as Inspector of Elections in October of 1836, Pent began to assume a position of leadership in the community, which numbered near 100.

All the Pent men were mariners, but, like the other settlers on Key Vacas, the family also farmed to supply its members with fresh vegetables and fruits. In 1839, a visitor to Key Vacas began to interest them in a new type of farming, one with a commercial potential. The visitor was Dr. Henry Perrine, who had settled on Indian Key temporarily, awaiting the end of the Seminole War. Perrine came to Key Vacas to treat the sick, but while there, he spoke in glowing terms of his plans to establish a settlement on the mainland devoted to raising commercially useful tropical plants and urged the settlers to experiment with the seeds he gave them.

At first, the settlers were not persuaded by Perrine's arguments and continued to devote their efforts to growing edible plants such as melons, squash, and sweet potatoes. But Pent and William Whitehead were impressed by the possibilities and, in 1840, each of them planted a dozen mulberry plants and a pint of Sea Island cotton seeds. Perrine was hopeful that the example of these two leading citizens would encourage the rest of the Bahamians, who, by 1840, numbered near 200, to follow suit and ulti-

Captain Temple Pent Sr. circa 1860
(courtesy of Eugene R. Lytton Sr.)

mately become settlers on his mainland grant.

But all of Perrine's dreams, as well as his life, came to an end on August 7, 1840 in the Indian raid on Indian Key. When news of the attack reached Key Vacas, most of the settlers again fled to Key West, and many of them did not return even after a small naval detachment was stationed there for their protection. The Pents, however, were among those who remained despite the Indian threat.

With the destruction of Indian Key, Key Vacas became the population center of Dade County. Pent, with his eleven children, was a principal contributor to the community's growth as well as its leading citizen. In 1841, he was elected delegate to the territorial House of Representatives and served three successive terms. In 1845, he was elected to represent the Southern District of Florida in the territorial Senate.

After nearly forty years at sea, Pent decided to try shoreside life for a while. Through his connections in Tallahassee he secured appointment, in 1848, as principal keeper of the Cape Florida Lighthouse on Key Biscayne, an important post in those days. During the four years he served as lightkeeper, he maintained his residence on Key Vacas and, in 1854, reentered politics in an unsuccessful run for the state Senate.

In the meantime, the population of Key Vaca, which was about forty in 1850, had continued to dwindle and, by 1860, was reduced to six families of Pents and one single man. Pent was again at sea, as were his four sons and a son-in-law. In 1866, he was reappointed principal keeper of the Cape Florida Lighthouse and remained at that post until his death in 1868 at age seventy-four. The name of Temple Pent Sr., squire of Key Vacas, stands out among early rural Keys pioneers as that of a man devoted to the interests of his fellow settlers. A memorial plaque in his honor stands at the entrance to the Museum of Natural History of the Florida Keys on Key Vaca.

Happy Jack – Happy Farmer Meets an Unhappy Fate

The memory of one of the lower Keys' more colorful pioneers is preserved in the name of a tiny mangrove island called "Happy Jack Key" located just off the northeastern tip of Sugarloaf Key.

Happy Jack, whose real name was Jonathan Thompson, was a pre-Civil War settler who had a plantation on the eastern shore of Sugarloaf Key across the channel from Cudjoe Key. A coast surveyor's report which makes reference to "Happy Jack's Point or Kay" and to a "Happy Jack Inlet" indicates that he settled there sometime before 1849. Another surveyor's report in 1856 notes that Happy Jack's plantation was producing "various tropical fruits and excellent sweet potatoes."

Stories about Happy Jack come from two different sources. One is a writer who visited Sugarloaf Key and wrote an article that appeared in *Putnam's Monthly* magazine in December 1856. The other source is an article based on an interview of descendants of William Baker, who, according to family legend, was a friend and neighbor of Happy Jack.

According to the *Putnam's Monthly* article, Happy Jack, before settling on Sugarloaf Key, was a member of a band of happy-go-lucky men who wandered all over the Keys, living wherever and however they were able to. It was probably during this period of his life that he acquired the nickname "Happy Jack."

Besides Happy Jack, the band included Jolly Whack, Paddy Whack, Red Jim, Lame Bill, and Old Gilbert. As the writer put it, "However different their names and varying dispositions, they all united in a common love. The fragrant goddess of whiskey absorbed the affections of their guileless hearts."

Lacking any ready source of their favorite beverage in the wilds of the Keys, the band had to sail to Key West to replenish their stock. The article continues:

> They necessarily went down sober, for the want of liquor sent them; but it was no less a matter of course that they should return drunk.

77

Skillful sailors as they were, and favored by Providence with moderate breezes and smooth seas oftener than they deserved it, nevertheless, it sometimes happened, that the winds blew and the waters rose, just when their skill deserted them. Three or four such mischances thinned their numbers rapidly, till, at length, only Jack was left.

Jack was always disinclined to the world, and Key West probably did not elevate his opinion of human nature. So he settled himself permanently on the key [Sugarloaf] we have just described and bent his energies to trapping deer and raising fruit. He is still alive, and likely to live. His solitude is not so uncompromising as Robinson Crusoe's, for the crowds of spongers and fishermen that swarm around all the keys give him sufficient company, indeed more than he deserves.

Actually, Happy Jack had less than two years to live after the publication of the *Putnam's Monthly* article. While that article implies that he lived alone on Sugarloaf, a family legend has it that he had a friend and neighbor by the name of William Baker.

The Baker story agrees that Happy Jack was a loner and refused to go to Key West. He would ask passing fishermen and spongers to bring him supplies and would, according to Baker's descendants, pay them in gold coin. Naturally, Baker wondered where the gold coins came from, but Happy Jack would never tell him and took pains to avoid being followed when he went off to his supposedly secret cache in the woods.

The soil in the Indian Mounds area, formerly the site of a Keys natives' village, was rich, and both Baker's and Happy Jack's plantations were productive. But they had a problem. Key deer would get in among the fruit trees and eat the blossoms and the new leaves.

A commonly used anti-deer device among the early settlers was called a spring gun. A gun would be rigged alongside a deer path in such a manner that when a deer hit a trip wire stretched across the path, the gun would fire. Baker and Happy Jack rigged a spring-gun beside a deer path leading to their plantations. Incredibly, they forgot where they had placed it.

One day, as they were walking side by side along a path, they tripped the wire. Both men were felled by the gun's blast. Baker, the taller of the two, was wounded in the calf, while Happy Jack was hit in his hip. Despite his own wound, Baker managed to get his friend into his sailboat and take him to Key West. It took the better part of a day before they arrived, and by that time, Happy Jack was unconscious from loss of blood.

Happy Jack died soon after their arrival, never regaining consciousness and perhaps the chance to tell his friend where his gold coins were hidden. Baker and his descendants have searched for them in vain.

Both stories contain some elements of truth. As we know from the survey-

Happy Jack and his companions – "it sometimes happened that the winds blew and the waters rose just when their skills deserted them" (*Harper's New Monthly Magazine* No. CVL, April 1859, courtesy of University of Miami, Otto G. Richter Library)

ors' reports, there was a man called Happy Jack and he did have a plantation on Sugarloaf Key during the 1850s. His real name, according to the 1850 census, was Jonathan Thompson. But at that time, he did not live alone. Two men, both listed as mariners, lived with him. One was James Anderson, age seventy, who might have been the "Red Jim" of the original happy band. The other was a young man, Robert Johnson, who later married and moved to Cudjoe Key. In the records of deaths at the St. Paul's Episcopal Church, Key West, there is the following entry, "May 2, 1858 'Happy Jack' name unknown about 60 years old." According to the writer of the Baker story, there was a tombstone in the Key West cemetery, since disappeared, that bore the inscription, "Died by accident . . . John Thompson . . . May 1st, 1858 . . . a native of England." The full, true story of Happy Jack will probably never be known, but his name will live on forever as the name of a little key not far from his plantation home.

Chapter 6

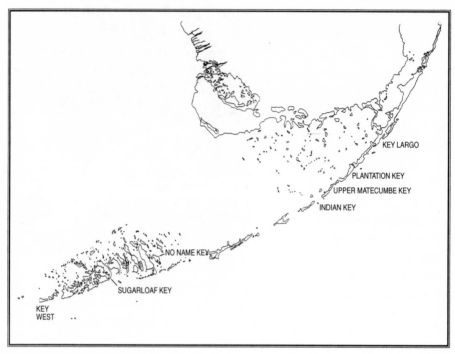

Post–Civil War settlements

PINEAPPLES, DILLIES, AND CHARCOAL

(1865 – 1904)

In the rural Keys, the period between the end of the Civil War in 1865 and the start of survey work for the Overseas Railroad in 1904 was marked by a continuing influx of immigrants from the impoverished Bahamas and the rapid rise of pineapple cultivation in the upper Keys. Five years after the end of the war, largely as a result of the Bahamian immigration, the population of the Keys outside of Key West had increased almost fourfold to a total of 300.

In 1870, every major Key in the lower Keys was occupied. Out of a total of 132 settlers, slightly more than half were farmers engaged in raising fruits and vegetables for the Key West market. Nearly all the rest were seamen on wrecking, freight-carrying, and fishing vessels. But by 1880, most of them had given up and the lower Keys were nearly deserted. After 1880, black Bahamians began moving into the lower Keys; by 1900, they outnumbered their white neighbors two to one. Most of the late-1800s lower Keys settlers eked out a living cutting firewood and making charcoal for the stoves of Key West. The rest farmed, fished, and gathered sponges.

The middle Keys were the least populated during the post–Civil War period. From a high of thirty-four in 1870, their numbers dwindled to ten by 1900. Like their lower Keys neighbors, middle Keys residents were mainly farmers and seamen.

The highly profitable pineapple farming industry in the upper Keys resulted in an increase in the population from 245 in 1870 to 450 in 1900. The appearance of occupations such as teacher, minister, and postmaster in the 1900 census showed that the upper Keys were beginning to emerge from backwoods status.

With rare exceptions, the rural Keys settlers did not own their land. After the Keys were surveyed to establish township, range, and section boundaries in the early 1870s, a few settlers acquired title to their property under the Homestead Act, but most continued on as squatters on government land.

Spurred by the rise of the cigar-making and sponging industries, Key West grew to be the largest city in Florida in the late 1800s. With a population of 18,000 in 1890, Key West provided a large, readily available market for the produce of the rural Keys farmers, fishermen, and charcoal makers.

Settler's sloop offloading produce and charcoal to be sold at Key West market (courtesy of Monroe County Public Library)

By 1900, there were approximately 600 people living in the Keys outside of Key West. The great majority were Bahamians or of Bahamian descent, and three-fourths of them were living in the upper Keys, engaged in raising pineapples.

"Old Ben" Baker – Wrecker Begins Pineapple Boom

Capt. Ben Baker, a Key West wrecker whose success earned him the title "King of the Wreckers," is generally credited with being the first to raise pineapples commercially in the Keys. Described as "tall, gaunt, shrill-voiced, hook-nosed, and hawk-eyed," he was as successful with his pineapple raising as he was with being the first to the scene of nearly every major wreck.

Around 1866, Old Ben, as he was known, imported 6,000 pineapple slips (suckers cut from the stalks) from Cuba and planted them on his Key Largo property. We read of him earning $7,000 from his 1871 crop and announcing that he would have 50,000 to 60,000 pineapples ready for sale from his 1876 crop.

News of Old Ben's success spread rapidly, and soon new settlers were clearing hundreds of acres of dense woods in the upper Keys to start plantations. A typical pineapple plantation would have a cluster of plain wood buildings near the shore in the shade of a coconut palm grove. These were the quarters of the overseer and workers, the packinghouse, and storage buildings. The workers' houses were tiny shacks, painted white if painted at all. Wooden shutters over the window openings were tightly closed at night to keep out the mosquitoes.

To clear the dense woods, planters used the slash-and-burn method. Field workers cut down the trees and bushes, left them lying where they fell, and, when they were dried out, set them on fire. The fields ranged in size from 10 to 100 acres. They were criss-crossed by rocky paths which provided access for weeding and harvesting.

Pineapples were grown from slips or from sprouts cut from ripe pineapples. Laborers planted the slips in the ashes wherever there were patches of soil among the outcroppings of rock, about 10,000 to the acre. They weeded the fields until the plants became so thickly intertwined as to prevent any further weed growth.

Scenes at a Keys pineapple plantation: 1. A pineapple grower's residence 2. A pineapple grower in field attire 3. Cutter working with a smudge [fire] 4. A file of "toters"
(from "Pineapples of the Florida Keys" by Kirk Munroe, *Harper's Weekly*, Aug. 22, 1896)

About two weeks before the pineapples were ripe, black Bahamian workers called "cutters" harvested the "pines." The cutters wore thick shoes, heavy canvas suits, and gloves to protect themselves from the poisonous spines on the pineapple leaves. Because harvest time was also mosquito season, they also wore nets over their heads and worked in the smoke of smudge fires set at intervals throughout the fields.

Despite the minimum care and shortage of rain, the pineapples thrived. An acre of land would generally yield about 7,000 pineapples in eighteen months. After the fruit was cut, the roots would yield a second and, usually, a third crop. No fertilizer was used, but after four or five crops, the field would be exhausted. It was then abandoned and allowed to return to its natural state.

The profits were considerable. According to one source, as much as $2,000 could be realized from the yield of a single acre. Amos Lowe of Key Largo shipped a schooner load of 36,000 pines to New York in 1876. In 1877, his son Leonard planted 1,000 acres on Key Largo. A Plantation Key planter anticipated a crop of 96,000 in 1880; in 1882, another plantation expected to ship 480,000 pines.

One of the major problems facing planters was getting the pineapples to the northern markets before they spoiled. Black Bahamian workers called "toters" carried the green fruit on their heads in sacks or baskets to the waterfront. A basket contained four or five dozen pines and weighed between 200 and 250 pounds. One gigantic toter named Black Caesar was reputed to be able to carry a 500-pound load.

At the waterfront, the toters loaded the pines into small sailing dinghies which carried them out to schooners waiting at anchor in deeper water. The smaller schooners transported the pines to Key West, where they were reloaded aboard north-bound steamers. Larger, clipper-lined schooners, some built especially for the trade, sailed direct from the plantations to Baltimore, New York, and other northern ports. With favorable winds and the Gulf Stream, they could make the voyage in eight or ten days.

On one voyage, the fifty-one-foot schooner *Irene*, owned and captained by the famous wrecker Bradish "Hog" Johnson, loaded pineapples from plantations on Key Largo and Elliott Key and sailed slowly out into the Gulf Stream with a light breeze. That night, the wind freshened from the southeast and sent *Irene* bowling northward with the lee rail nearly under. Five and a half days later, with the lee rail still awash, Hog made his landfall on Barnegat Light, New Jersey.

Such fast runs were the exception rather than the rule. Often, calms or storms would delay the vessel, the pineapples would overripen, and the planter would suffer a heavy financial loss.

Some of the wealthier planters purchased and operated their own schooners to minimize shipment delays. They also built long docks out to deep water, or dredged channels into their docks so that they could load directly from shore.

On the average, about twenty-five percent of the pines would spoil during shipment. This problem was greatly alleviated when, in 1896, the railroad reached Miami and shallow-draft steamers began providing three-times-a-week service between the plantations and Miami during the harvest season.

A devastating hurricane struck the Keys in 1906 and destroyed most of the pineapple crop. It was the beginning of the end. The hurricane was followed by a blight.

Six years later, freight cars on the Overseas Railroad, once viewed as the answer to the Keys planters' prayers, were rolling by filled with pineapples, but not those grown on the Keys. The freight cars were stuffed with pineapples grown in Cuba by cheap labor and transported across the Straits of Florida on Henry Flagler's railroad car ferries. It was the ultimate irony as the Keys planters watched them roll by their fields. By 1915, all commercial pineapple growing in the Keys had ceased.

Nicholas Matcovich – Hermit Farmer of No Name Key

One fact about pioneer life in the Keys stands out above the rest – only a handful of the early settlers were able to endure the rugged, isolated life for more than a few years. One notable exception was a man named Nicholas Matcovich, who settled on No Name Key in 1868 and died there fifty-one years later at age ninety-two.

The story of Matcovich is a fascinating one in both its facts and its legends. An enigma, Nicholas was married to the same woman for fifty-four years, fathered seven children and yet, for forty-three of those years, lived as a hermit. Hospitable and kind to the few people who knew or met him, yet he supposedly surrounded his property with gun traps to kill unsuspecting intruders.

Born of Russian parents in Austria in 1827, Nicholas immigrated to the United States when he was twenty-one and became a citizen eight years later, in 1856. Nothing is known of his early years in the United States beyond the fact that he lived in New Orleans and supposedly served on Confederate blockade runners during the Civil War.

The war's end found Nicholas in Jacksonville, Florida, where he married Eliza Ann Carey, a twenty-year-old Bahamian girl eighteen years his junior. Attractive but uneducated, Eliza, like many other Bahamian immigrants, could neither read nor write.

With the end of the Civil War, the lucrative blockade-run cotton trade came to a halt and the Bahamas sank into a depression. Hundreds of near-starving Bahamians immigrated to Key West and the Keys to find a better life. Shortly after they were married, Nicholas and Eliza moved to Key West to join some of Eliza's Bahamian friends and relatives already living there.

In Key West, Nicholas managed a nursery but was not happy. The booming post-war population of Key West was approaching 5,000, and Nicholas did not like crowds. Farming was in his blood. He craved a place of his own where he could grow things and not be bothered by a lot of people. At that time, some Bahamian immigrants were settling in the lower Keys to farm, fish, or sponge. Encouraged by their example, Nicholas and Eliza gathered together their meager possessions and set sail for No Name Key in 1868.

A small island, approximately one by two miles, and about thirty miles from Key West, No Name Key was the site of the largest post–Civil War settlement in the lower Keys. In fact, with forty-five settlers and twenty-three dwellings, No Name Key had more people and houses in 1870 than it did in 1990. All the heads of household, except Nicholas, were Bahamians.

Nicholas staked out a tract of land bordering the eastern shore of the island. He built a tiny twelve-by-fifteen-foot, one-room driftwood house; dug a well; and constructed a crude dock for their sailboat.

His next task was to clear the land for planting. The heat, mosquitoes, and almost impenetrable undergrowth, coupled with hidden rattlesnakes, made this a miserable, backbreaking, and hazardous job. However, Nicholas was more than equal to the challenge. Short and stocky, with what were described as "enormous hands," he was a very strong man and, further, he was doing what he knew and loved best.

As soon as enough land was cleared and fenced to keep out deer and raccoons, Nicholas planted sweet potatoes and other vegetables to feed himself and Eliza. After clearing more land, he planted fruit trees and cash crops such as melons and squash to be sold at market in Key West.

The results of Nicholas's hard work were reflected in the 1870 census report. Of the ten farmers on No Name Key, he had by far the highest-valued real estate. The value of his land, buildings, and cleared acreage was recorded as $1,000, compared to the next highest farm property valuation of $400.

In the seven years since they arrived, Eliza had given birth to three boys, and the original house had become crowded. To make more room, Nicholas built a second, slightly larger house measuring fifteen by fifteen feet.

A serious blow to the family's fortunes came in the form of a hurricane in October 1876. One account of this hurricane said that "it flooded the Keys and destroyed most of the houses." Nicholas's houses were damaged, his dock was washed away, his crops were ruined, and many of his fruit trees were destroyed.

To make up for the losses they had sustained, Eliza went to Key West and began working in a cigar factory. When work was slack and on holidays, she returned to No Name to visit her family. In addition to needing the money, Eliza was glad to get away from the isolation and loneliness of No Name Key. She was not alone. Her neighbors, fed up with the mosquitoes, the heat, the shortage of water, and the poor soil, were rapidly deserting the Key.

In 1881, by which time Nicholas had cleared eighty acres and fenced thirty of them, he submitted his claim for a homestead grant of 160 acres. Two former neighbors, Thomas and William Knowles, supported his claim. In their affidavits, both men downgraded the value of Nicholas's property. Thomas said, "The hurricane injured his place greatly. One hundred dollars would pay for the place now." William was even more deprecating. "I wouldn't give much for the place as the land is poor and exposed to hurricanes."

As the years passed, Eliza's stay in Key West became permanent and her children joined her. But she continued to visit her husband from time to time and gave birth to four more children. Only one, a girl, survived. The last child, who lived only a year, was born in 1895 when Eliza was fifty and Nicholas was a sixty-eight-year-old grandfather.

During the 1880s and '90s, Key West was a hotbed of Cuban revolutionary activity. Money was raised to fit out expeditions to send troops and arms to Cuba clandestinely. Some of these filibustering expeditions, as they were called,

Nicholas Matcovich in his 60s. (courtesy of Patricia Warren, Nicholas's granddaughter)

used the Keys as hiding places or rendezvous sites. According to one of his grandsons, Nicholas was involved in filibustering. Supposedly as payment for his part in the risky business, Nicholas received a small fortune in gold coins, which he buried on his property.

One of the few firsthand sketches of Nicholas's character comes from a letter written in his behalf by a No Name Key neighbor in 1899 to help Nicholas get a clerical error in his land patent corrected. The neighbor, obviously a well-educated man, explained that Nicholas had been a bonafide settler on No Name Key for thirty-one years and is "solely a farmer – not a sponger, wrecker, coal burner, or land pirate – he has improved his land and is an upright, honest man who should be assisted, encouraged, and protected. For it is such men ' . . . that make the wilderness blossom as the rose.'"

Nicholas and his neighbor accompanied a government land agent during his investigation of conflicting land claims on No Name Key. In his letter, the neighbor goes on to say, "As an example of his [Nicholas's] innate courtesy and kindness of heart, I will state that, as the Keys are famous for rattle snakes, he persisted in walking ahead of your [the government's] agent and offered to accompany him in the field to protect him without fee or hope of reward."

89

In the late 1890s, Nicholas took in a boarder, a black Bahamian named Samuel Hamilton, to help him on the farm. Now in his seventies, Nicholas was still a strong, healthy man, but, as a result of his self-imposed exile on lonely No Name Key for more than thirty years, had become increasingly withdrawn and suspicious of strangers.

Although it seems out of character for a man who walked ahead of a land agent to protect him from rattlesnakes, Nicholas is reported to have placed trip-wired guns around his property. Whether he actually did this or merely advertized that he had is in question. There are certainly no reports that anyone ever set off one of the guns or was injured.

In 1904, Henry Flagler gave the go-ahead to start construction of the Overseas Railroad. William J. Krome, a brilliant young engineer who later became the chief construction engineer for the entire project, was initially in charge of the survey work.

When, in early 1905, survey parties reached the lower Keys, Krome met Nicholas. Despite his desire to live alone and be left alone, Nicholas had gained a reputation as a skilled and successful fruit farmer. He planted and nurtured a wide variety of tropical fruits, including sapodillas ("dillies"), and performed experiments to develop new strains.

Krome was as much or more interested in commercial horticulture as he was in railroad construction. He and some associates had started a citrus grove in what was to become Homestead while he was still building the railroad. Impressed by Nicholas's work, he took the opportunity when he was in the area to visit the No Name Key farm and inspect the results of Nicholas's experiments when he was in the area.

Robert Watson, a farmer on Big Pine Key in the area today known as Watson's Hammock, owned a large sailboat which he used to carry his own and other settlers' produce to market in Key West. On his return trips, he would deliver food staples and other supplies needed by homesteaders. One of his customers was Nicholas.

In her memories of her girlhood days on Big Pine Key, Robert Watson's daughter, Mizpah Watson Saunders, recalls Nicholas as "an old man by the name of Nichols." Through her recollections, we gain another firsthand picture of Nicholas, his lonely life, his fears, and his basically kind heart.

She writes:

He was a strange sort of man. He did not trust anyone. There were two signs to the back of his land. One read, 'Read and Run. If you can't read, run anyway.' The other read, 'Blow the horn (he had a conch shell horn there) or beat the drum (a wash tub), one step further and you will be killed.' He grew many vegetables on that land.

We went there one Sunday to deliver his supplies from Key West – he always let my father come ashore. This Sunday, he gave my father a big pot of calico beans and some hot, homemade bread which he had baked on banana leaves, and we ate it while still sitting in the boat. It was most delicious! Then to our surprise, he told us we could go ashore, so we did. He would only let us children stay on the beach, but invited my mother and father to go in the house with him. After that he treated us all very good.

News of the wonders worked by the hermit fruit grower on No Name Key continued to spread. In 1908, a reporter succeeded in gaining Nicholas's confidence, toured his farm, and wrote an article which appeared in the *Key West Citizen* newspaper under the title, "Fruit Farming on the Keys – A Visit to the Matcovich Plantation on No Name Key." The writer argued that the proper direction for future development of the Keys was fruit farming rather than "fishing clubs, sporting organizations and private residences" for the wealthy.

From this article, another picture of Nicholas appears: that of a hardworking, intelligent, and highly skilled horticulturist. The article continues:

It [Nicholas's farm] is an example of what may be accomplished on the chain of keys, with profit and enduring value, by any intelligent and industrious person. He has been on this farm consisting of 120 acres about forty years, and in the latter half of his residence has laid out most of it in tropical fruit trees, comprising more than twenty-five varieties, some of them entirely new to this section and many of them of considerable rarity. With a market, such as will be opened after the advent of the railroad, this kind of permanent development of the keys should become the most profitable occupation of the soil.

Much of the success of such a variegated stock depends, as in the case of the Matcovich fruit farm, on an intelligent care and development of the trees. That he is an expert in such matters is evident from his skilled grafting and budding, and the results of experimentation with fruit new to these sections. His work is recognized, and has been highly complimented, by the Agricultural Department, and he has been repeatedly asked for specimens of his fruits for exhibition at Washington.

In October 1909, a severe hurricane struck the Keys. Damage to railroad construction equipment and embankments was heavy, causing months of delay and millions of dollars of additional costs. Mizpah Saunders recalled that the water flooded almost all the way across Big Pine Key, destroyed most of their house, and washed away all their furniture except the big iron stove. There is no record of the damage suffered by Nicholas, but, judging by what happened on neighboring Big Pine Key, it was undoubtedly extensive.

The following year, another October hurricane hit the lower Keys. The storm lasted for thirty hours, washed away railroad embankments, and even blew down a cigar factory in Key West. Once again, Nicholas's farm suffered heavy damage. He was saved from near starvation only by food packages sent to him by his benefactor Krome, now chief engineer in charge of building the Overseas Railroad.

After the double hurricanes, Hamilton, Nicholas's hired hand, departed, leaving him alone again. Now in his eighties, Nicholas continued to cling to his land and his beloved fruit trees. With occasional visits from his children in Key West, who brought him some supplies, he managed to keep going.

In 1912, the year the railroad was completed, David Fairchild, a well-known horticulturist and father of Fairchild Tropical Gardens in Miami, toured South Florida via the Overseas Railroad and Key West. Enroute, he stopped in Marathon to see Krome. Fairchild was as much, or more, interested in Krome's citrus grove in Homestead as he was in the engineer's railroad-building feats. In the course of their discussions, Krome told Fairchild about the old Russian fruit farmer on No Name Key who was growing sapodillas "as big as saucers." Fairchild was eager to see the dillies, as the natives called them, so Krome took Mr. and Mrs. Fairchild by launch to No

Name and Nicholas's farm. In his book, *The World is My Garden*, Fairchild describes Nicholas as "a picturesque old fellow, with a great shaggy beard, large head, and perfectly enormous hands."

Continuing his description of the visit, Fairchild goes on to say:

In a haphazard way, he had planted patches of fruit trees and vegetables, and as he was particularly fond of sapodillas, he had many trees of this delicious fruit. More than once he had nearly starved to death and doubtless would have done so had it not been for Mr. Krome's kindness in sending him food from time to time.

He was morbidly suspicious and set gun traps in the brush, stretching invisible wires about, so that visitors to the Key were in danger of being shot. As we were with Mr. Krome, we were received with great cordiality and even allowed a peep into his shack, which was incredibly disorderly and unkempt.

Fairchild-Krome visit to Nicholas Matcovich in 1912, left to right: David Fairchild, Mrs. Fairchild, William Krome, Nicholas Matcovich (in doorway), unknown man (courtesy of Monroe County Public Library)

93

To Fairchild's dismay, the sapodillas he had come to see were not in fruit.

The final sketch we have of Nicholas is as he was in 1916, just three years before his death. It comes from Ethea Stricker, who at the time was a young schoolteacher holding classes on No Name Key for four months of that year. Ethea's boyfriend, whom she later married, was a young man named George Stricker, who worked at the First National Bank in Key West.

Strange as it may seem, Nicholas had an account at the bank and George Stricker handled his account. Stranger still, despite his supposed unfriendly disposition, Nicholas permitted George to bring Ethea and her twelve students to his place for a visit. The schoolteacher recalls it this way:

> The house was built on stilts and the walls were covered with guns of every kind. This must have been his hobby. It was very rough, one room with an oil stove and a bed. Mr. Mac was very nice but the house and his appearance were eerie. He was married and had a wife and family in Key West, but preferred the life of a hermit.

The last few years of Nicholas's life are shrouded in as much mystery as the rest. His wife died in Key West in 1917 at the age of seventy-two. About the same time, Annie, who was Nicholas's favorite child, and her husband, Henry Leon Sands, a sponger, moved to No Name Key, perhaps to be near Nicholas.

According to another family story, Nicholas, shortly before he died, told Sands the location of one of his buried jars of gold coins and promised to tell him the location of the rest on his next visit. Unhappily for the family fortunes, Nicholas died on August 14, 1919, at the age of ninety-two without revealing the rest of his secret. Together with his supposed treasure trove of gold coins, Nicholas Matcovich, the hardiest Keys pioneer of them all, lies buried in his beloved land on the island he was never willing to leave.

Woodcutters and Charcoal Burners – Forgotten Pioneers

For more than 100 years, a handful of forgotten men labored in the dense, mosquito-infested woods of the lower and middle Keys to keep the housewives of Key West supplied with wood and charcoal for their stoves. The majority of these woodcutters and charcoal burners (people who made charcoal) were black Bahamian immigrants, who usually lived alone or with one or two other woodmen in crude driftwood shacks.

As the population of Key West grew, the island's supply of wood suitable for stoves was soon exhausted. One of the first suppliers of wood to Key West was Henry Geiger of Boca Chica (see his story in Chapter 5). Henry employed a sixty-three-year-old black man named Robert Allen to cut the wood which he sold for $3.50 a cord in Key West in the 1850s.

The best-burning wood was buttonwood, a dense, hard wood from trees that grew near the shoreline on most of the Keys. A Keys traveler in the late 1800s reported, "A log of buttonwood, when set on fire at one end, will burn to ashes before the fire goes out and generate an intense heat." Buttonwood was also used to make charcoal and — according to some sources — makes the best charcoal of any wood in the world.

The first charcoal burner for which there is any record was George Wilson, the sole inhabitant of Big Pine Key at the time of the 1870 census. Unlike most of his successors, George was a white man. The 1870 census also listed two woodcutters, both on Sugarloaf Key.

As might be expected because of the growing Key West population, the 1880 census showed a significant increase in lower Keys charcoal burners and woodcutters. There were thirteen charcoal burners, all but three of whom were black men, and six white woodcutters. The 1900 census reported only seven charcoal burners and no woodcutters, but ten years later there were twenty-four "woodmen" living between Cudjoe Key and No Name Key and nine men who were both spongers and charcoal burners in the middle Keys.

The process of making charcoal was a long, arduous, and lonely one. While buttonwood was the preferred wood, other trees such as the red mangrove could be used.

After locating a thick stand of suitable trees, the charcoal burner cut them down, trimmed the branches, and "stood up" a kiln in a cleared area. He constructed the kiln by stacking the logs in a tentlike structure, leaving a small opening at the top. He set up the large logs first, followed by suc-

Charcoal kiln; according to Setson Kennedy, who took this picture in 1939, this is "the largest charcoal kiln ever 'stood up' on the Florida Keys, approximately 25 feet in diameter and 12 feet high, it will yield over 200 sacks of charcoal." (courtesy of Stetson Kennedy)

cessively smaller limbs. Next, he covered the entire structure with a thick layer of grass or seaweed, followed by a layer of sand or dirt.

From a separately started fire, the burner picked up glowing coals and dropped them into the kiln through the opening in the top. He closed the opening with more wood, grass, and sand, forcing the heat to spread throughout the interior. The kiln had to be tended day and night to keep it burning slowly and evenly and to prevent the fire from breaking through at any point. The burner maintained control by strategic placement of more sand or dirt.

Depending on the size of the kiln, it would take three to ten days to reduce the wood to charcoal. During that period, the charcoal burner, if he did not have a helper, or did not live nearby, had to remain at the site, catching short catnaps on the ground or in a crude shelter.

After the charcoal had cooled, the charcoal burner packed it in sacks and loaded it aboard small sloops for transport to Key West. A cord of buttonwood would yield about ten sacks, and a typical sloop could carry about 150 sacks.

Some idea of the extent of this trade can be gained from the narrative of a Keys cruise made in 1885. The author reported passing, in one day, eight sloops outbound from Key West, all engaged "in the stovewood and charcoal trade with the Island City."

Charcoal burning did not completely die out with the advent of gas and electric stoves in Key West. Many Key Westers, particularly those of Cuban ancestry, enjoyed the flavor that buttonwood charcoal imparted to roasted meat, and at least one Key West coffee mill used the charcoal to give a distinct flavor to its Cuban coffee.

A few charcoal burners continued to build their kilns even into the years after World War II. One of the last of them was Bertram Cash, a black man who came to the Keys from the Bahamas when he was seventeen. Bertram burned his last kiln on Cudjoe Key in 1960, having made charcoal for forty years.

Today, those with the energy and the interest to fight their way through some of the dense buttonwood growths in undeveloped sections of the lower and middle Keys may come upon a large circular area of barren ground, a reminder of the lonely, backbreaking, mosquito-infested days of the charcoal burners.

Chapter 7

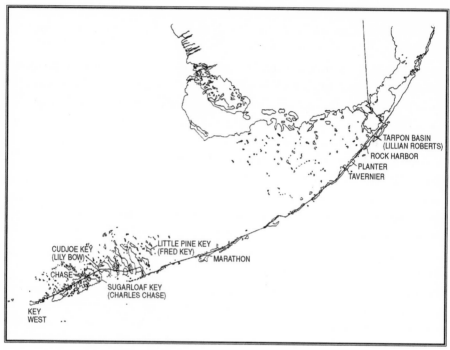

Railroad-era villages and homesteads

RAILROAD DAYS

(1905 – 1922)

*T*he isolated way of life of the Florida Keys pioneers neared an end when, in 1905, construction of the Overseas Railroad began. Seven years later, on January 22, 1912, the first train from the mainland rolled into Key West, and an umbilical cord was formed upon which Keys dwellers were to become ever more dependent.

The simple Bahamian farmers, spongers, and charcoal burners looked on silently as hundreds of workers flooded onto their islands and began cutting wide swaths through the mangrove forests and hardwood hammocks. By the second year of construction, there were more than 2,500 of them. The natives watched as millions of cubic yards of rock and fill were dumped into the shallow waters to form railroad embankments across the water gaps that separated them from their neighbors. They gazed in amazement at strange-looking craft – Mississippi River stern-wheelers, floating derricks, and barge-mounted pile drivers – that appeared over the horizon and began building bridges across the wider and deeper channels.

The few hundred settlers wondered what the railroad would mean to them. Most expected it would make their lives easier by bringing mail almost to their doorsteps; by making a trip to buy supplies, visit relatives, or see a doctor a matter of hours instead of days; and by greatly reducing the danger of spoilage in shipment of their farm produce.

But not all the rural Keys inhabitants were happy. The farmers and woodmen saw hundreds of acres of good farmland and fine hardwood hammocks destroyed. Captains of Keys sailing craft cursed the railroad as the channels connecting the Gulf and Atlantic sides of the Keys were closed and access to sheltered storm anchorages between the Keys was blocked forever. Spongers and fishermen looked on with dismay as the muddy waters from dredging and bridge construction spread over their favorite sponging and fishing grounds and ruined their take.

Then, in October 1906, a hurricane killed more than 130 railroad workers, severely damaged railroad beds and construction equipment, and ruined upper Keys pineapple plantations. It was a setback from which the planters never recovered. A blight, two more hurricanes, and, finally, competition from the cheaply produced Cuban pineapples drove them out of business. By 1915, no more pineapples were being grown for commercial purposes in the Keys.

Primarily as a result of the demise of the pineapple plantations, the population of the rural Keys shrank during the railroad construction period from about 600 in 1900 to about 450 in 1910. In the lower Keys, the majority of the inhabitants were blacks engaged in cutting wood and burning charcoal for the stoves of Key West. The rest were small truck farmers or boatmen. The few settlers in the middle Keys, half of them blacks, were engaged mainly in sponging, fishing, and charcoal burning. In the upper Keys, planters who did not leave turned to raising limes, tomatoes, melons, and other truck-farm produce.

By 1908, the railroad had reached Knight Key at the western end of Key Vaca, and regular service was begun. A small city of storehouses, shops, offices, living quarters, and even a hotel sprang up on Key Vaca. Known as Central Supply, it was the nerve center of the gigantic construction project and the birthplace of present-day Marathon.

Two more hurricanes, one in 1909 and another in 1910, struck the Keys. The 1909 storm killed forty workers, washed out forty miles of railroad embankments, and convinced the railroad engineers to replace many of the embankments between the Keys with bridges. Profiting from the experience of the hurricanes in 1906 and 1909, railroad crews were ready when the third storm hit in 1910, and only one life was lost.

While the big news was the damage to the railroad and the loss of life among its workers, these hurricanes, and another in 1919, also severely damaged settlers' houses, crops, and boats. But the rugged Conchs rebuilt, replanted, and hung on to their island homes. With the coming of the railroad, other signs of civilization, such as post offices, stores, schools, and churches, began to appear on the more populated Keys. Swelled by railroad employees, by new ventures such as sponge farming, and by an infant tourist industry, the rural Keys population began to grow again, reaching nearly 800 in 1920.

For the farmers, the railroad was not as much of a blessing as they had hoped. Produce from northern farms was shipped by rail into southern Florida, and the demand for Keys-grown fruits and vegetables began to fall off.

Pigeon Key children greeting Overseas Railroad train
(courtesy of Monroe County Public Library)

The railroad also brought in a new industry which was totally unnoticed by the farmers, spongers, and woodmen but many years later would become the mainstay of the Keys economy. A few fishermen had begun acting as sport fishing guides for visiting yachtsmen as early as 1902. In 1908, the Florida East Coast Railway Company began construction of a luxurious resort, the Long Key Fishing Camp. It attracted famous and wealthy sportsmen from all over the country and served to promote the construction of more rural Keys resorts in the '20s and '30s.

In 1917, the first move toward what would eventually become the Overseas Highway was taken. A bond issue was approved to construct "trails" (single-lane dirt roads) on Key Largo and Big Pine Key; to build a bridge from Key West to the next island to the east, Stock Island; and to build a short road on Stock Island.

While the railroad had brought the outside world much closer, it did little to change the daily life of the typical Keys settler of the early 1900s. Many still lived in crudely built one-room houses. There was no electricity or running water and few of the children attended school. Keys farmers continued to plant, cultivate, and harvest their crops by hand, and many of them continued to transport their produce to Key West by sailboat. The spongers and fishermen also continued to use sailing craft, although a few who could afford it added auxiliary engines. And the lonely, backbreaking labor of the charcoal burners remained unchanged.

Lily Bow – Lady Pioneer on Cudjoe Key

Bow Channel, which runs between Cudjoe and Sugarloaf keys, gets its name from a remarkable pioneer lady who lived on Cudjoe Key from 1904 to 1906.

In the summer of 1904, Richard and Lily Bow and their two young sons stepped ashore to survey their newly acquired property on the western shore of Cudjoe Key. Purchased from a previous homesteader, their new home consisted of 207 acres of part pine and hardwood hammock and part marsh and salt pond. There was a small cabin, and several acres were cleared and planted with lime trees. Key West, the nearest outpost of civilization, lay twenty miles to the west, reachable only by sailboat. The only other inhabitants of the island were several black families engaged in making charcoal.

Strong-willed, independent-minded, college-educated Lily had urged her booze-loving husband to quit his job with the City of Chicago Engineering Bureau in order to start their lives and marriage over again in the wilds of the Florida Keys. Lily, who loved the outdoors and growing things, had been told by an acquaintance that it was possible to make a good living raising limes and cotton in the Keys. Richard reluctantly agreed to give it a try.

Lily Lawrence Bow (courtesy of Mary Bow, Lily's granddaughter)

On the property they found cotton growing wild and sent samples to the Department of Agriculture in Washington. The Department reported back that the cotton was of good quality, but the project was never pursued. After a few months of the heat, mosquitoes, and the lack of any liquid refreshment other than water, Richard packed up and departed.

Left to fend for herself with Douglas, age four, and Lawrence, age fourteen, a lesser woman would have given up and gone home to relatives or friends. But not Lily Bow. She was not a quitter and did not mind in the least being on her own.

Their home was a one-room, weather-beaten, board-and-batten cabin raised off the ground on three-foot-high posts. Solid wood shutters could be closed to cover the glassless window openings during storms. Inside, curtains divided the room into sleeping and living-room areas. An upright piano and a china closet filled with Lily's favorite tea service were in sharp contrast to the otherwise plain furnishings. From a small porch at the back of the cabin, a covered walkway led to a lean-to cookhouse where a crude grill constructed of limestone rock served as a stove.

Just beyond the cookhouse were two small storage sheds, a chicken coop, and a vegetable garden planted with tomatoes, yams, and melons. Nearby, a shallow well yielded sometimes fresh, sometimes brackish water, depending on rainfall. The well water was normally used only for watering the garden and washing. Drinking water, often in short supply, was obtained from rain-water barrels fed from the roof of the cabin.

For the first six months after he left, Richard sent money, but, in June 1905, he transferred title to the Cudjoe property to Lily and that was the last the family ever heard of him. Lily was now almost totally dependent on her own resources to feed herself and her two boys. The family supplemented the vegetables and fruit they grew with foods provided by nature on the island and in the waters around it. Lawrence gathered wild honey, set traps, and hunted deer in the woods. In their small sailboat, he caught fish, set turtle nets, and gathered shellfish. But there were times when the traps were empty, the fish not biting, and the vegetables or fruit not ripe, and the little family went hungry.

Rattlesnakes, alligators, panthers, and poisonwood trees were minor concerns compared to the hordes of mosquitoes and sandflies, or no-see-ums, that came with the hot, rainy weather. At times, the mosquitoes came in clouds so thick they would blacken the side of the cabin. Lily and Lawrence built smudge fires of mangrove branches to envelope themselves in a protective cloud of smoke when they were working in the garden and the lime tree grove. They covered the open windows of the cabin with cheesecloth, but the cloth blocked out the breeze as well as the mosquitoes. Lily also burned pyretheum powder, made from dried chrysanthemums, inside the cabin to hold the insects at bay. At night, everyone slept under mosquito netting.

Periodically, Lily and the boys sailed to Key West to sell their limes, eggs, and surplus vegetables and fruits at the market. With the cash earned, they purchased essential supplies such as salt, sugar, flour, coffee, and kerosene.

As her grandchildren expressed it, Lily "never met a stranger," and she made good friends of the black families who were her only neighbors on Cudjoe. The nearest white neighbors were the Bullards, who lived across the channel on Sugarloaf Key. Lawrence and Douglas found friends among the ten Bullard offspring, and the children visited back and forth by boat.

There was no school in the lower Keys, so Lily held classes for her own boys and the Bullard children in her cabin. News of a "schoolmarm" on Cudjoe spread to neighboring Keys and soon other settlers' youngsters and even some adults were coming to Lily's "school" to learn to read and write. In payment, they gave fruits, vegetables, fish, and venison. One teenage girl told Lily that she had to be able to read and write so she could beat out a more-educated rival for her beau's affections – and she did.

When her boys became ill or were injured, Lily had to rely on her own resources. She had a bottle of "Wizard Oil," the universal remedy of the times for everything from a toothache to the flu. In the garden she grew aloe for cuts, burns, and stings. Her black Bahamian neighbors taught her the remedies available from native trees and plants. These included seeds, called "purge nuts," of the tallowood tree for a laxative; berries of the stopper tree for diarrhea; and a brew from gumbo limbo bark for intestinal upsets.

Despite the hardships and hazards of life on Cudjoe, Lily found happiness in the challenge. During a newspaper interview some thirty years later, Lily, speaking of her days on Cudjoe, said she "loved every minute of it."

In February 1905, surveyors for the Overseas Railroad began working on Cudjoe Key. Their boss, William J. Krome, was a young engineer who later assumed direction of the gigantic construction project. The surveyors were amazed to find a lone, educated lady and two boys living in such an isolated place. When they told Krome about Lily, he resolved to meet this unusual woman. Not long thereafter, Krome's motor launch made its way up the channel and docked at Lily's homestead.

Bill was impressed by Lily's obvious education and cultural refinement, as well as her courage and determination to make a go of it on her own. From that moment, a friendship began which was to last the rest of their lives. Bill visited Lily on other occasions when his work took him near Cudjoe. As he came to know her better, he became increasingly concerned about the hardships she had to endure and the scant living she was able to make.

For another year, Lily continued to eke out a living on isolated Cudjoe. On one of his visits, Bill Krome told her that soon a construction workers' camp would be built on Sugarloaf Key across the channel from her homestead. After that, hundreds of roughneck railroad workers would be working on Cudjoe just a few hundred yards from her cabin. Concerned for Lily's safety, Bill urged her to leave before they arrived. Lily was not ready to give up. She had worked very hard and thought she could see the day when her lime grove would begin to pay off. Further, she had no money and no place to go. On a subsequent visit, Bill offered to give Lawrence, about to turn sixteen, a job with the railroad and arrange to have the family moved to Miami. Reluctantly, Lily accepted his offer.

Just a few days before the devastating hurricane of October 1906 struck the Keys and killed more than 100 railroad workers, Lily and her boys said goodbye to their island home. After a brief sojourn in Miami as a music teacher, Lily turned to pioneer life again, this time in the wilderness that was to become Homestead. On a homestead grant, she built a log cabin, cleared the land, and planted a citrus grove. Lily lived in Homestead nearly all the rest of her life. She helped organize the Women's Club, and started a library which eventually became the city's public library, named the "Lily Lawrence Bow Library" in her honor. In 1929, she was honored by the Lion's Club as the "outstanding citizen of the Redlands District."

In her sixties, Lily found that running the library, playing piano in an orchestra, managing her citrus grove, and performing various civic functions were not enough to keep her occupied. In her remaining days, she wrote several books of poetry, published a poetry magazine, and wrote a newspaper poetry column. Among her works is this poem of her memories of Cudjoe Key.

CUDJOE

There's a little island named Cudjoe,
I lived there once . . .
It was all so long ago . . .
No dreams of a highway to link
The archipelago
With a North land some called "The States."
The keys all jade and emerald green,
A chain of precious jewels
Laid on a sea of ultramarine

Blue, a different shade of blue
From any color known to artist's brush,
It somehow holds the light of dawning day,
The sparkle of the sun, and yet the hush
Of evening when the sun has gone,
And sometimes a frothy white lace
Swirls and foams along the keys
Till blown to spray it vanishes.
Sometimes the setting sun
Turns all the blue to ruby red and gold,
To frame the unchained jewels.
    And sometimes all the sea is gray and cold.
Sometimes a stormy fanfaron[1]
Beats his way across this jeweled sea
And sweeps away the sand and stone
Leaving only mangrove roots to catch and hold
Bits of flotsam and tiny coral things
So lands may build anew.
    I lived there once . . .
It was all so long ago . . .
But memory keeps alive the buttonwood
And slender tree fern . . .
The crimson seeded pomegranate
That grew near by the quern,[2]
That old hand-mill
Where we ground our grits and meal.
The shadowy path leading straight
To the sea where smoky tern
Come in to feed.
The home-made grill,
A place to cook our bread and fish.
And always, night and day

---

[1] Storm.
[2] Hand mill for grinding grain.

107

The swish . . . swish . . . and swish . . .
Of water. Porpoise
Romped about like children playing hide
And seek . . . and . . . seek . . . through
The ebbing, flowing tide.
    And I remember
The arm of the sea that seeped
Its way inland to the lake [3]
Where black boys burned the charcoal
And loaded it on boats. At daybreak
They sailed away to 'Tinka.'[4]
The sisal hemp pole reached high
And marked the place to watch for sails
Billowing against the sky.
The tree snails
With gay colored coats,
The smell of burning pyretheum[5]
Making smudge . . . the steady, buzzing hum
Of mosquitoes.
And at early dawn the sandfly
Pushed sleep away. And with the rising sun
Birds awoke and sounded reveille.
    It was all so long ago
But the flavor of sea purslane[6]
Lingers still to recall those days of hunger
Which dragged so slowly by.
A hurricane . . .
Witch-hazel with its yellow bloom.
The healing power of thick, juicy leaves
Of Aloes so bitter to the taste

---

[3] Large saltwater pond in northwestern part of Cudjoe.
[4] Probably refers to Key West, where all charcoal was sold.
[5] Powdered dry chrysanthemum, a mosquito repellent.
[6] A fleshy-leaved trailing plant used by settlers in salads and to flavor other foods.

Yet soothing to a fevered skin. Sheaves
Of cotton and tobacco growing wild.[7]
 Bleached bones of black-fish
Traced some early flood. Trails aisled
By deer on forage hunts,
And often in the night
A shrill cry of panther
Woke us from our dreams, not in fright,
For who could find aught to fear
Living close to Nature's Heart,
As we did here?
 I saw strange men[8] come in
And measure off each mile
And write black figures on white stakes,
Then go away awhile . . .
Then return to build a span
Across the blue . . .
The things I remember were all so long ago,
But I lived there once . . .
On a little island named Cudjoe.

     —Lily Lawrence Bow

Charles Chase — English Playwright to Sponge Farmer

Chase, Florida, once the fastest-growing community in the Florida Keys and the site of an industry that promised to become one of the most lucrative in the state, is gone and forgotten. The only evidence of this former settlement on Sugarloaf Key is a two-story, white clapboard house and concrete disks, relics of the sponge industry, occasionally found on the bottom of the Sugarloaf sounds.

---

[7] Wild cotton was once common in the Keys. It was eradicated in the 1930s to prevent the spread of the bollworm to cultivated cotton.
[8] Railroad surveyors.

In the short space of four years, Chase grew from a single house to a community of nearly 100 people and then suddenly plunged from a $100,000 enterprise to bankruptcy. The story of its rise and fall is a fascinating tale of great expectations and dashed hopes that took place in the lower Florida Keys before World War I.

The story begins in the 1880s, when two men – Jeremy Fogarty, a Key West sponge buyer and packer, and "Commodore" Ralph Munroe, a pioneer settler of Miami – conducted separate experiments in artificial sponge cultivation. Fogarty's results in the lower Keys and Munroe's in Biscayne Bay indicated great promise for the process.

Seventy-five percent of Munroe's planted sponge cuttings survived and doubled in size in six months. But both men were plagued by the same problem: sponge poachers who would descend on their underwater farms and steal the nearly mature sponges.

Munroe and Fogarty tried to get the state legislature to set aside a small area in Biscayne Bay in which they could continue their experiments protected from poachers. But when it was discovered that the senator who introduced the bill had a financial interest in the project, passage was defeated, and Munroe and Fogarty abandoned their efforts.

The next sponge-cultivation experimenter was Dr. J. Vining Harris, a wealthy Key Wester who owned all of Sugarloaf Key except the southern shore. In 1897, perhaps at the instigation of Harris, the state legislature passed an act which granted people the right to plant and propagate sponge in waters adjacent to their land and to have police protection over the beds of planted sponge. Although the act was repealed two years later, a special provision allowed all those who obtained sponge-cultivation rights under the original act (that is, Harris) to retain them.

The large, nearly landlocked, shallow sounds at Sugarloaf Key provided an ideal site for sponge-cultivation experiments. They had large areas with the right depth, about three to five feet, they could be protected from poaching, and they were relatively undisturbed by strong currents or winds. Harris began experimenting there in 1897, but there are no records of his results. About 1901, he turned over the use of his property, and the house he had built, to Dr. F. H. Moore, head of the U.S. Department of Fisheries, to continue the experiments.

Moore was familiar with the methods used and the results achieved by

Cultivated sponge grown on concrete disk (courtesy of Monroe County Public Library)

Fogarty and Munroe. Building on their work with ample government funding and resources, he pursued various cultivation methods over the next several years. In 1908, he published a report concluding that artificial cultivation from small cuttings of natural sponges was feasible and practical.

He stated the following principal requirements for success: (1) do not plant where there is freshwater intrusion or a sandy bottom, (2) protect from poachers, (3) fasten cuttings from natural sponges to concrete disks with aluminum wire (which would slowly dissolve), and (4) plant in shallow water.

He reported that the cultivated sponges grew round and smooth and were superior to natural sponges because they did not have to be torn from the bottom and did not contain imbedded particles of coral and sand.

At this point in the story, two Englishmen, Charles Chase and his brother George appeared on the scene. Born and raised in England, the Chase brothers came to America as young men to pursue their separate careers. George became a businessman and settled in Chicago, while Charles made his way into the theatrical world, first by writing plays and later by producing and sometimes acting in them.

In 1899, Charles brought his touring company to Key West. Both he and his actress wife fell in love with Key West and spent the summer there. During his next visit to Key West in 1906, Charles chanced to meet Moore and learned about his sponge-cultivation experiments. Charles had soured on show business because of a huge flop he had produced in 1904. Intrigued by thoughts of an entirely new venture, he kept in touch with Moore after going back to New York. When the news of the doctor's success arrived, Charles persuaded his brother George to go into the sponge-growing business with him.

The Chase brothers came to Key West in January 1910 to inspect the Sugarloaf property and start negotiations with Harris to buy it. They formed the "Florida Keys Sponge and Fruit Company" (they also planned to raise key limes) with themselves and an English friend, Henry Bate, as majority stockholders.

Charles then journeyed to England to raise more capital from well-to-do friends and relatives. A major influence on prospective investors was the fact that, at the time, the combined sponge harvests of the Keys and Tarpon Springs were insufficient to supply the demands of domestic, let alone foreign, markets.

Upon Charles's return, the deal was concluded, and Harris sold his Sugarloaf property to the Florida Keys Sponge and Fruit Company for $45,000. George returned to his business in Chicago, while Charles and his family moved to Sugarloaf to begin the enterprise.

To start a totally new industry in the mangrove wilds of Sugarloaf Key in those days was a tremendous undertaking, and the obstacles facing Charles were many. Although construction of the railroad right-of-way had been completed, there were, as yet, no tracks, and train service would not commence for almost two years.

Everything from heavy construction materials to food and medical supplies had to be brought by boat from Key West. Because the sounds were shallow and the entry creeks narrow, only small boats could be used.

The only existing facilities were Harris's house and several small cabins and a dining hall left from the railroad construction era. These were only a fraction of what would be needed to house a work force that would grow to sixty employees. There was no electricity and no telephone. Fresh water came from a few shallow wells and rainwater was collected from roofs.

Charles, his wife, and a fourteen-year-old niece moved to Sugarloaf Key in the spring of 1910. His twenty-four-year-old son, Charles (Pete), joined the family in August. The Chases took up residence in the three-bedroom stilt house that Harris had built. Since they were isolated from society and tormented by the heat and mosquitoes, it is a wonder that this well-born, artistic, and talented English gentleman stuck to his task. Only a powerful and compelling dream of the riches to be reaped with the first sponge harvest held him there.

A group of laborers from Key West began clearing the land, digging wells, erecting water storage tanks, and constructing additional living quarters and facilities for processing and planting sponges. These workers lived in the cabins originally built for the railroad construction crew.

The workers enlarged the stilt house by adding a living room. Next, they constructed a two-story building with an office and company store downstairs and three bedrooms upstairs. They added a high wooden tower on one side of the office building to serve as a lookout tower for spotting sponge poachers.

As spring progressed into summer, more laborers were hired until the work force consisted of approximately forty men, the majority blacks, some of whom brought their families with them. By this time, the construction crew had completed building the factory where concrete disks, to which the sponge cuttings would be attached, would be manufactured. (The disk factory was located in the vicinity of today's Sugarloaf Lodge). Production of the ten-inch-diameter, one-inch-thick disks began that summer.

Construction of facilities and manufacture of disks continued into the fall, but sponge gathering (for the cuttings) had to wait for the arrival of cooler weather because of the risk of the sponges dying in the hot water while awaiting transshipment and planting.

A near disaster struck the little community one day in October. The winds began to increase and by late afternoon reached hurricane force. Driven by powerful gusts from the north, water began piling up on the low-lying land. By nightfall, the workers' cabins were flooded and they were invited to take refuge in the Chase house, which stood on six-foot stilts. Segregation was still the order of the day. The white workers and their families were allowed to come inside, while the black workers and their families stood huddled together on the porch on the house's lee side.

As night wore on and the wind howled louder, the water continued to rise until it was within a foot of the floor, or about five feet deep. The upper half of the lookout tower blew away and there were fears the stilt house would go next. But at 3:00 A.M., the winds and the water level began to subside, and by the break of day, the workers were able to slog back to their cabins through an inch of white silt, which now covered the entire island.

By November, all was ready for beginning operations. Two sponge schooners, each manned by a crew of ten, sailed to the Marathon area to gather the natural sponges. Marathon was selected because the lower Keys sponge beds had been largely depleted.

The spongers gathered sponges in the usual manner, using a glass-bottomed bucket and a long pole with tines to tear the sponges off the bottom. To keep the sponges alive, they immediately placed them in live wells in the dinghies. When the wells were full, the spongers rowed back to the schooners. There, crewmen cut the sponges into smaller pieces and wired them to long wooden slats. They then inserted the slats into wooden torpedo-shaped storage bins and submerged the bins alongside the schooner.

Every three or four days, a launch would arrive to tow the bins with harvested sponges back to Sugarloaf. The schooners remained on the sponge grounds for about a month before returning to Sugarloaf for resupply.

The Sugarloaf planting crews began work as soon as possible after a load of sponges arrived. They operated from planting barges, platforms mounted on pontoons. Vertical poles at the sides of the barges, called "spuds," were used to move the barge and to anchor it in place as needed. A submerged enclosure of wooden slats, called a "live boat" and mounted between the pontoons, held the sponges underwater until they were planted.

Just prior to planting, the crew cut the sponges into smaller pieces about the size of a hen's egg and wired them to the concrete disks with aluminum wire through two holes in the center of each disc.

The barge crew planted the sponge disks in rows spaced about thirty feet apart. They could plant between 300 and 500 sponge cuttings in a day. As they walked the barge along a planting line with the spuds, a man tossed the disks into the water using a spinning motion to ensure that they would sink with the sponge side up. Water depth had to be three feet or greater; in shallower depths, the sponges would die when the water became too hot.

At the end of March, gathering and planting stopped because of the onset of hot weather. The work force was reduced, and those who remained manufactured disks and constructed additional housing, shops, and storage buildings. They also planted and tended fruit tree groves and vegetable gardens, and assisted in other experimental agricultural projects.

Sometime during the second year, 1911, a railroad construction crew of more than 100 men arrived on Sugarloaf to complete the work of laying the track. A bunkhouse mounted on a barge was towed in and moored at what is today called Harris Gap.

In January 1912, track laying was complete and the great day when Henry Flagler would ride over his "own iron" into Key West was at hand. For the occasion, the Sugarloaf workers decorated the disk factory, which stood close to the tracks, with red, white, and blue bunting. A man took station in the lookout tower to signal the approach of the train. When he cried "smoke ho!" all the workers dashed down to the tracks and waved and cheered as the great man rode by.

Disc factory at Sugarloaf Key decorated for arrival of first Overseas Railroad train; sign on top of building reads: "Chase," lower sign reads "F. K. S. & F." for Florida Keys Sponge and Fruit Co. (courtesy of Monroe County Public Library)

Two years after its establishment, the sponge-cultivation settlement had grown into a small town with a peak work force of sixty and a population approaching 100. There were now concrete houses for the workers, a store, a boat repair shed, a refrigeration plant, marine ways for hauling boats, stables for two horses, lime and fig tree groves, a vegetable farm, and wonder of wonders, a telephone.

With the Overseas Railroad running by the front door, regular mail service became a possibility. Charles submitted an application to establish a post office and, soon after, the name "Chase, Florida" became official.

Chase had a store, a post office, a telephone, and even an ice plant, but the town lacked one important element: a police force. The sponge workers were happy and easygoing, and managers did not expect any problems with them; they were more worried about the prospect of sponge poachers coming into the sounds. Accordingly, Charles arranged to have his son Pete appointed a deputy sheriff. No one, least of all Pete, ever expected he would be called on to do more than chase poachers.

The railroad construction crewmen were a rough lot, many of them derelicts from the slums of northern cities. Liquor was forbidden in the railroad camps, but some enterprising natives always managed to find a way to turn a profit by bootlegging booze to the workers. The inevitable result of mixing liquor with the boredom of camp life was fighting among the men.

One night, a breathless railroad worker rushed into the Chase house to report that one of the men had killed another in a fight. Pete strapped on his gun and ran to the bunkhouse. Fortunately, the murderer, now sober, was sitting peacefully, waiting to be taken into custody. His victim was quite dead. One of the workers described the final blow this way: "He cut him wide, and deep, and permanent." Pete handcuffed the man and, lacking a jail, locked him in one of the stables overnight. The next morning, Pete flagged down the train and escorted his prisoner to Key West.

In addition to sponges and key limes, Charles conducted other cultivation experiments. A headline on the front page of the March 6, 1912, *Key West Morning Journal* announced, "Sugarloaf Cotton Beats All Others." The article reported that samples of sea-island cotton grown by the Florida Keys Sponge and Fruit Company had been examined by the Department of Agriculture and found to be the best submitted in a period of three years.

Charles also experimented with growing agave, which yields sisal, a strong cordage fiber. While he proved that he could grow both crops successfully, he also discovered that, because of high labor costs, they could not be competitive in the marketplace, and he abandoned the projects.

Sometime during his second summer at Sugarloaf, Pete went with the launch to Key West to obtain supplies. At the Curry & Sons dock, he met some young lawyers who were talking about having a beach party, so Pete invited them to bring the outing to the beach at Sugarloaf.

The following Sunday, the north-bound train stopped in front of the disk factory and disgorged a laughing group of young men and women. Among them was a lovely blonde woman named Hattie Johnson. Pete was instantly smitten by her beauty and began a long-distance courtship which culminated in their marriage in 1913.

Amusements for young people on isolated Sugarloaf were limited, consisting mainly of outdoor activities such as fishing, swimming, beach parties, and sports contests. To have more daylight available for recreational activities after work, the town of Chase ran on its own time, setting clocks ahead one hour in summer and two hours in winter.

Pete and Hattie were an adventuresome couple, and supplemented the sports activities with more ambitious ventures of their own invention. Sometimes they rode a railroad hand-car the thirty miles to Marathon to play tennis with the railroad engineers. Once, they hiked to Key West over eighteen miles of railroad ties.

On another occasion, they set off for Miami in a sailing canoe with a small tent and folding cots. After three days of sailing and paddling against contrary winds, they had gotten no further than Big Pine Key, and decided to abandon the voyage. Dragging the canoe and gear to the railroad track, they flagged down the midnight train and persuaded the amazed conductor to let them put the canoe in the baggage car and drop them off at Sugarloaf.

By 1913, sponges with three years' growth were beginning to near commercial size. But instead of waiting another year or two, when they would be ready for harvesting, the stockholders of the Florida Keys Sponge and Fruit Company voted to take a gamble calculated to vastly increase their profits.

They decided to retrieve, cut up, and replant the three-year-old sponges. They estimated that each partially mature sponge would yield about ten cuttings, and when these were fully grown, the firm would be able to produce approximately two million sponges a year.

At first, the local natural-sponge gatherers paid scant attention to the operations at Sugarloaf, but as news of the project's apparent success and anticipated huge yields became known, the spongers became concerned about its effect on their livelihoods. Some attempts were made to poach the growing sponges, but Pete had no trouble scaring off the poachers with verbal warnings or shots over their heads.

Moore had concluded, from his sponge-growing experiments at Sugarloaf in 1908, that the sponges would grow to commercial size in about four years. But at the beginning of 1914, it became evident that five or six years' growth was needed for the sponges to reach maturity. With their capital nearly depleted, the Chase brothers returned to England to raise more money.

They succeeded in soliciting enough money to continue operations for two or three more years. But fate intervened. Before they could transfer the money to America, World War I broke out. All of the firm's major stockholders were British subjects, and the funds they had put up, on deposit in a London bank, were frozen. The Chase brothers returned to America empty-handed.

There was nothing to do but shut down the business and hope the war would end soon. The labor force was released and Chase, Florida, became a ghost town, its only residents the Chase families senior and junior.

An effort was made to revive the sponge-cultivation business by selling shares to American investors wintering in Florida in 1916, but the northern tourists were more interested in buying real estate than sponge futures. In May 1917, The Florida Keys Sponge and Fruit Company was declared bankrupt and the business and property were sold to Miami Beach real estate salesman R. C. Perky for $200,000 (see Chapter 8 for the story of Perky).

No sponges other than samples were ever harvested or sold. After Pete moved to Key West in 1916 and his father followed him in 1917, sponge poachers began to invade the sounds and steal any sponges that had matured. In 1917, a sponge blight wiped out the natural sponges in the lower Keys and also the cultivated sponges in the northwest and southwest Sugarloaf sounds.

Fred Key – Tomato Farming on Little Pine Key

Little Pine Key is one of the larger islands not connected to the mainland by the Overseas Highway. It is located about a mile and a half north of No Name Key and about three miles east of Big Pine Key.

Uninhabited and overgrown today, Little Pine was, in the early 1900s, nearly half cleared and farmed by a handful of settlers. Among them was a large family with nine children, consisting of one girl and eight boys. Their name was Key and this is the story of their life on Little Pine as recalled by Frederick Key, the next to youngest of the boys.

Sometime in the 1800s, an Irish sailing captain named Key was shipwrecked near Nassau in the Bahamas. The captain settled there, married and had a son whom he named Thomas. In the 1880s, the son emigrated to the Keys, where he met and married another recent arrival from Nassau, a small, dark-haired girl named Emma Johnson.

Captain Tom, as he came to be called, was a big strapping man who was a sponger and fisherman. Both he and Emma were hard-working, thrifty individuals. In time they saved enough money to buy the captain his own boat and later to purchase a house in Key West.

Around 1910, a friend of Captain Tom's named Jimmy Knowles, who had a farm on Little Pine, boasted to Tom about the fertile soil on the island and told him an eighty-eight-acre homestead site was available.

The Overseas Railroad was then two years away from completion. When it was finished, it would be possible to ship vegetables and fruit grown in the Keys to northern cities without danger of their spoiling. The demand for fresh produce in the wintertime in the north was growing, and Captain Tom sensed that here was a moneymaking opportunity.

Recognizing the difficulties of starting from scratch on a small island thirty miles from Key West, Captain Tom nonetheless decided the potential rewards were worth the effort. Everything the eleven-member family needed on that isolated island, including building materials, house furnishings, provisions, and farm implements, had to be transported in the captain's small sailboat from Key West. They had to build a house, dig wells, and clear, till and plant the land. Every member of the family, except the very youngest, pitched in until they finally had a roof over their heads and seed for the first crop in the ground.

Keys tomato grower (from estate of Lester Dubell, courtesy of Matecumbe Historic Board)

Fred Key was two years old when the family settled on Little Pine. By the time he was old enough to remember, there were five farms in addition to their own. Three were white farmers and two were black. There were no other children and only one other woman.

Like most of their neighbors, the Key family did not stay on the island year round. They would arrive in October to begin planting and stay until the voracious hordes of mosquitoes drove them away at the beginning of the summer. On the twelve acres they had cleared, they planted tomatoes and watermelons.

When planting was finished, Captain Tom and one or two of his older sons resumed sponging and fishing. They were usually gone for two or three days and sometimes as long as a week. While they were away, the oldest remaining boy took over running the farm with the help of the other children. About once a month, the family sailed to Key West to restock.

Their house had two rooms. A small room was the parent's bedroom. The larger room served as the kitchen, sitting room, and sleeping quarters for the nine children. Later, when the oldest child, Flossie, was married, another room was added for the newlyweds. Kitchen facilities consisted of a wood-burning stove and a large washbasin.

Outside the house, Emma had a dutch oven built of rocks. The children hauled fresh water in buckets from two nearby shallow wells. Contrary to the experience of many early Keys settlers, the water from the wells was always adequate and never brackish.

The fertile soil and surrounding woods and waters provided the Key family with a bountiful supply of food. In their vegetable garden they grew sweet potatoes, okra, black-eyed peas, and sweet peppers. Sapodilla trees provided a delicious dessert, and Key lime trees furnished juice to make "old sour" to flavor their fish. They kept a few pigs for their own consumption, and raised a large flock of chickens, both to be sold in Key West and to supply the family with eggs and meat.

Other sources of fowl for the table were the many white-crowned pigeons, doves, herons, and cormorants that inhabited the island. Guided by the sound of their croaking, the boys would locate the nests of young cormorants in the mangrove trees and knock them out with a long pole. Wading in the shallows, they were able to catch spiny lobsters and gather conchs with ease.

A favorite treat was turtle meat, particularly green turtle. The boys would anchor a net about thirty feet long in the "turtle hole," a deep-water spot near the island. They aligned the net with the direction of current flow rather than across it to avoid having it fouled by floating weeds and grass. The turtles normally swam back and forth across the current, and in so doing became entangled in the net. The boys checked the net twice a day until a turtle was caught.

They kept the turtle alive until Captain Tom returned home and butchered it. Emma pickled in brine the meat not eaten immediately. She then prepared a favorite family feast by placing alternate layers of turtle meat and dressing in a deep bowl, topping it with thick tomato sauce, and baking it in the outdoor oven.

Sometime after the land was cleared and planted, Captain Tom constructed another building which they called the packinghouse. After the boys harvested the tomatoes, they carried them to the packinghouse where Emma would sort them according to size and quality while the smaller children wrapped them and packed them in crates. Captain Tom loaded the crates aboard his twenty-eight-foot sloop, appropriately named *Tomato*, and sailed to Big Pine Key. There he loaded the crates on the next train going north.

The Key children attended school on No Name Key. No Name had one of the larger populations on the islands of the lower Keys. (To put this in perspective, the 1910 population of No Name was twenty-two, and that of Big Pine was seventeen). On school days, the family ate an early breakfast of grits and eggs, and the younger of the nine children embarked in two dinghies, accompanied by their mother or an older brother. Each dinghy was about fourteen feet long. They sailed or sculled, depending on wind conditions, across Big Spanish Channel to No Name Key. The distance to school, located on the southern shore, was about three miles.

While the children were at their lessons in the building, which also served as the church, their mother visited with friends. By 1918, No Name Key was settled by about fifteen families who engaged in fishing or farming or both.

When school was over in the early afternoon, the mother and children sailed back to Little Pine, but if the weather had suddenly deteriorated, they spent the night with friends on No Name. Back home after school, the children devoted most of the rest of the day to chores such as hauling water, pulling weeds, and feeding the chickens and the pigs. Fred Key recalled that his favorite chore was chopping wood for the stove.

Every night before supper, the children took baths in two large washtubs in the pig house. The nearest doctor was in Key West, so for most injuries and illnesses, the family relied on patent medicines and pioneer remedies. Occasionally, more serious medical problems arose, and it was necessary to go to Key West by boat, which took the better part of a day.

Because of a lack of medical knowledge and readily available medical aid, one of the boys lost his sight in one eye after it became infected. The family had tried home remedies, but when Captain Tom returned from a sponging trip, it was apparent that the remedies were not working. He immediately set sail for Key West with the boy, but by the time they arrived, it was too late to save his sight.

On another occasion, however, a pioneer remedy proved superior to the doctor's prescription. Captain Tom had a kidney ailment and nothing the Key West doctor gave him seemed to help. One day, his neighbor Charlie Knowles told Captain Tom he knew of a cure. Tom followed Charlie into the pine woods and watched as Charlie carefully selected a bunch of fresh pine needles. He crushed them and dropped them into a pot of boiling water. Tom drank doses of the resulting potion at regular intervals and, in a short while, his kidney problems disappeared. On his next visit to Key West, Captain Tom advised the doctor to get himself up to Big Pine Key and stock up on pine needles.

In September 1919, Captain Tom and four of his sons, including Fred, were on Little Pine while the other members of the family were away in Key West and Miami. Their first warnings of the approach of a storm were a rapidly falling barometer, increasing winds, and rain. Captain Tom immediately put the boys to work to secure the homestead. This included herding their 500 chickens into the house for safekeeping.

With his four sons aboard, Captain Tom ran the *Tomato* as far into a mangrove-lined cove as she would go and tied up to the mangrove trees. In darkness, shrieking winds, and stinging rains, they rode out the severe hurricane of September 9, 1919. A day and a half passed before they were able to get back to their homestead. The roofs on both the house and the packinghouse had been blown away and only one chicken had survived.

In 1923, the Keys were the only people left on Little Pine. The years of toil and isolation had finally broken Emma's spirit and energy. One morning as her husband was getting ready to leave on another sponging trip, she told him, "I'm tired, sick, and disgusted, and I want to leave this place." To her total amazement, Captain Tom said, "I've been waiting a long, long time to hear you say that." With that exchange, the Key family packed up and left Little Pine, never to return again.

Lillian Spencer Roberts — A Rough Beginning on Key Largo

Still alert and spunky at age eighty-five, Lillian Spencer Roberts recalled her girlhood days homesteading on Key Largo with these words, "What a life we lived! Daddy just drank and drank and drank and made Momma's life hell. Some days all we had to eat was pigeon peas. They were rough times."

In 1915, when Lillian was twelve, her father, William Spencer, moved his family from Homestead to Key Largo, where he obtained employment as a laborer on a key lime plantation owned by P. L. Wilson.

In those days, the population of Key Largo was approximately 250. There were small settlements located at Tavernier, Rock Harbor, Newport, and Key Largo. A severe hurricane in 1906, followed by a blight and the importation of cheaper Cuban pineapples, had ended the once prosperous pineapple industry and its principal center of activity at Planter. Most of the settlers were small farmers or laborers on plantations raising a variety of fruits and vegetables, principally key limes and tomatoes. Others were fishermen and railroad workers.

The Wilson plantation was near Rock Harbor. As Lillian remembers it, the settlement had a general store, a church, a railroad station, and about fifteen or twenty houses. The only vehicles she recalled were two trucks, owned by more prosperous farmers, which were used to carry produce to the railroad station, following a rough track alongside the railroad.

The Spencer children, except for the youngest, worked on the plantation pulling weeds and picking limes alongside their father. Lillian remembered the pain inflicted by the sharp thorns on the lime trees and being cheated out of her meager pay by the foreman's boys, who claimed the limes she picked as their own.

Two years after they arrived, a stroke of luck enabled Lillian's father to take over a 180-acre homestead near Tarpon Basin. The previous resident had been forced to abandon the place because, having no wife and no children, he could not qualify as a homesteader.

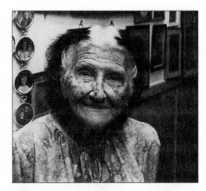

Lillian Spencer Roberts at age 85
(photo by Richard Watherwax)

The as-yet-uncleared property lay on both sides of the railroad tracks and had a small, one-room dwelling built on low stilts. Crowded into it were father, mother, Mizpah, sixteen, Lillian, fourteen, Corinne, twelve, Johnny, two, and baby Franklin. The family gradually cleared approximately three acres and planted tomatoes as their cash crop.

Inside the tiny house, a wood-burning stove and a large washtub in one corner served as a kitchen. The sleeping area for the children was separated from that of their parents by a blanket pinned to a clothesline. Kerosene lamps furnished illumination, and the bushes behind the house served as the toilet.

At first, the only source of water was from the Wilson plantation two miles away. The job of hauling water was assigned to Mizpah and Lillian. They filled water jugs at Wilson's place, put them in a cart, and pushed the cart home on a path alongside the railroad track. Sometime later, the girls found a sinkhole with fresh water beside an Indian mound on their own property.

Besides hauling water, Lillian was responsible for cutting wood for the stove. Despite her small frame, she boasted, "You better believe I could swing an ax! I used to chop down trees as big around as a barrel."

Around the homestead, the girls wore dungaree work clothes. Ankle-length dresses were reserved for school days and Sunday school. The girls scrubbed their own clothes on a washboard and pressed the dresses with a flat iron heated on the wood stove.

125

The family subsisted mainly on what they were able to grow, principally sweet potatoes, okra, and pigeon peas. Pigeon peas grew in long pods on bushes about eight to ten feet high. Similar in taste to black-eyed peas, they were eaten green or dried.

Lillian's mother made bread from sweet potatoes and johnny cake from flour. Sometimes there was not enough money to buy yeast, and the johnny cakes resembled sailors' hardtack.

The girls rarely had time to go fishing, but when they did, they would wade out waist deep in the water to cast their lines. Occasionally, Lillian's mother borrowed a rowboat from Mr. Charley, the foreman at the Wilson plantation, and took the girls out to deeper water. Lobster and conch brought welcome variety to their diet on the few occasions the girls had time to hunt them in the shallow water along the shore. A special treat was in store when a nearby settler caught a turtle and, as was the custom, shared the meat with his neighbors. There was no money for candy; as a substitute, the girls would boil crushed sugarcane to make a syrup and then let it harden.

When there was a little money available, mother and daughters walked to Rock Harbor to buy staples such as flour and salt and some canned goods. The nearest post office was at the village of Key Largo, almost five miles away. Despite the distance, the chance to accompany her father on a walk to Key Largo was a big adventure for Lillian.

The nearest doctor was at Homestead. When any of the family became ill, mother was doctor and nurse, and applied liberal doses of castor oil.

One of the few redeeming features of the house was that the doors and windows were screened. In the summer, the mosquitoes swarmed outside in thick clouds. Lillian said mosquitoes weren't swatted, they were scraped off in big gobs. To prevent them from getting in the house as people went in and out, the family kept a smudge fire burning in a big pot by the door.

Of greater concern were the numerous rattlesnakes likely to be found anywhere around the property. Panthers prowled the woods and, at night, would come up to the house and paw at the screen door. One moonlit night, Lillian, her mother, and Mizpah were walking home beside the railroad tracks. Lillian had gotten some distance ahead of the others when suddenly a big animal, seemingly white in the moonlight, reared up on its hind legs a few feet in front of her. Lillian yelled, "Go back, go back!" to her mother and sister. For an instant that seemed an eternity, Lillian and the panther stood frozen facing each other. Then Lillian picked up a rock and threw it at the animal. To everyone's great relief, the panther dropped to all fours, crossed the tracks, and disappeared into the woods.

The tomatoes grew large and tender in the rich, dark, leaf-mold soil. After they were picked, the children had to stay up all night wrapping them individually and packing them in crates. The next day, Lillian and Mizpah carried the crates to the railroad tracks, flagged down the train, and hoisted them onto a freight car.

Rube Goethe, a train engineer, often saw the girls pushing their cart filled with water jugs alongside the tracks and struggling to lift the tomato crates onto the freight car. His heart was touched. One day, after stopping the train, he said to the girls, "Your daddy should be ashamed. How sorry I am that you are not my daughters." He told them to get two old barrels, char the insides, and scrub them clean. "Put them beside the track," he said, "and when I'm going down [to Key West] with the water train, I'll fill them up." He also told the girls to build a platform of railroad ties to put the tomato crates on and he would take care of having them loaded onto the train.

School was a one-room, board-and-batten building on the Wilson place. The teacher, young Elise Warren, came from Key West and boarded with Wilson during the week. Among the eight students were two of Mr. Charley's boys, who were constantly playing mean tricks on the teacher and the other students. One day the teacher let Mr. Charley's boys give her a ride in a wheelbarrow. They climaxed the ride by aiming the barrow at a beehive and giving it a mighty shove. The teacher barely survived her bee stings, no other teachers could be persuaded to take her place, and that was the end of Lillian's school days.

As if hordes of mosquitoes, hidden rattlesnakes, and wandering panthers were not enough to contend with, there was the almost unendurable burden of an alcoholic, wife-beating, child-beating father. When the children got home from school, he would mark out an area to be weeded or cleared or planted before they could go play. Usually the task was so great that the children could never complete it. One day, when he told them to plant pigeon pea seeds by digging individual holes and placing three seeds in each, Lillian rebelled. At her instigation, the girls simply scattered the seeds over the ground and then ran down to the water to play. When the seeds sprouted and the father realized what the girls had done, he whipped them unmercifully with a leather strap fastened to a broomstick handle. When Lillian's mother protested, he growled, "If you get in the way, old lady, I'll give it to you too."

Lillian said she will never forget the fateful day when her father arrived home accompanied by a huge, fearsome-looking black man. He announced that the man would be living with them and working the farm on a crop-sharing basis. He claimed that his purpose was to relieve the family of some of the farm work, but, in fact, the only changes were that the room was divided by another blanket, there was less to eat, and the girls began to live in constant fear of being attacked. Lillian, determined not to be taken without a fight, slept with a machete by her side.

One person Lillian remembered with great fondness was Nick Pinder, who would come in his boat every Sunday to pick up the children and take them to Sunday school at the Methodist church in Rock Harbor. Another man who befriended the girls was the railroad section foreman at Rock Harbor who Lillian remembered as Mr. Cribbs. Cribbs would occasionally bring the family mail and gradually became aware of the way the children and their mother were being mistreated and their uneasiness over the presence of their intimidating boarder. He reported the situation to the local sheriff. One day, the deputy arrived on the Spencer doorstep. He ordered the boarder to pack up and leave and told Spencer that if there was another report of him laying a hand on Mrs. Spencer or the children, he would find himself sitting in a jail cell.

Among Lillian's few happy memories of her girlhood days were the rare times she got to ride the sixty-foot schooner *Island Home* to Key West and back again. The schooner left Newport around noon and, depending on wind and weather, arrived at Key West sometime the next day. There were no passenger accommodations as such; people just sat or lay down on deck. Lillian said the young folks would stay up all night telling stories and singing songs. "Sometimes it was rough, but it was great fun," she recalled.

Periodically in the dry season, sparks from locomotive stacks set fires in the hammocks near the tracks. One such fire proved to be Lillian's salvation. Joseph Roberts, a young railroad employee at Homestead, was dispatched to the Rock Harbor area to help put out a large hammock fire. He met Lillian and began courting her. One year later, she told her father that she and "Josie" wanted to get married. Spencer said he would kill them both first.

Plucky Lillian told her mother, "He's going to get his chance to kill me, because Josie and I are going to get married!" Her mother pleaded with Spencer to sign the marriage license and told him if he didn't, Lillian was going to run away. With that, the father finally relented.

Lillian and Josie were married in Key West and had fourteen children. After a long marriage, Josie died, leaving Lillian heart-broken but also with many loving memories of the fine life they had together after he rescued her from her misery at the homestead on Key Largo.

Inter-Keys freight/passenger schooner *Island Home*, built on Plantation Key in 1903; Lillian Roberts remembered her trips to Key West on board as sometimes rough, "but it was great fun."
(courtesy of Monroe County Public Library)

Chapter 8

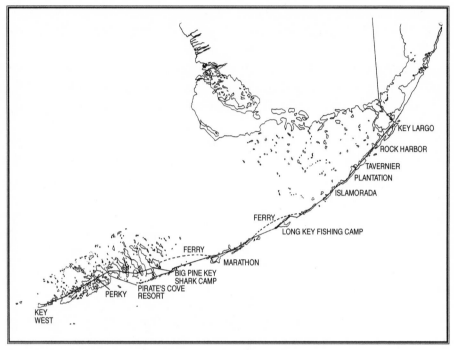

Early Overseas Highway days – ferry routes, villages, and resorts

A ROAD BEGINS, ANOTHER ENDS

(1923 – 1940)

*W*ith the dedication of the first Overseas Highway on January 25, 1928, the gates to the Florida Keys opened wide to the modern world. Service stations, lunch rooms, and tourist cabins soon followed the automobiles rolling down the Keys. Electric lights and telephones came much later, but by the end of the 1930s, a way of life that had remained essentially unchanged for more than a century was rapidly disappearing.

Construction of the highway began in earnest in 1923. At the time, most of the approximately 800 rural Keys natives were still making their living from the land and sea around them as farmers, farm laborers, fishermen, spongers, or woodmen. A few worked for the railroad, and a small number were employed by fishing camps such as the Long Key Fishing Club.

On the farms, the principal cash crops were key limes and tomatoes. The largest and most numerous of these were in the upper Keys. Their output was sufficient to justify the construction of a three-story packinghouse in Tavernier in 1928. In 1929, the Key Largo tomato crop was valued at $250,000.

Even as late as 1929, some community leaders were predicting that truck farming was the way of the future for the rural Florida Keys. Farmers tried a variety of fruits and vegetables, including bananas, coconuts, avocados, mangos, melons, okra, beans, and sweet potatoes. Unlike Key limes and tomatoes, none of these ventures met with great financial success.

Wood cutting and charcoal burning continued to provide livelihoods for a few black residents of the lower Keys. But as electric and gas stoves came into wider use in Key West, this occupation gradually died out.

Next in importance to farming were fishing and sponging. In fact, many farmers were also part-time fishermen and spongers. Marathon, with only about thirty residents at the time, became the principal fishing center when William (Pappy) Parrish opened a fish house in 1927. In the fall of 1927 and the spring of 1928, almost three million pounds of Spanish and king mackerel were shipped by rail from Marathon to Miami.

Another commercial fishing enterprise was shark fishing to obtain shark hides and shark liver oil. Several shark-processing facilities were in operation in the Keys at various times, but the largest and longest-lived was the Big Pine Key shark camp, opened in 1923 by Hydenoil Products. The story of its operation and eventual closing in 1931 is told later in this chapter.

The Keys farmers, fishermen, spongers, and woodmen continued to live very much as they had for decades before. Kerosene lamps, wood stoves, outhouses, and cisterns were the standard features of their simple homes. The only public electric power in the Keys outside of Key West in the 1930s was furnished by two small generating plants, one at Tavernier and the other at Marathon. In the late '30s, these plants supplied electricity to their immediate surrounding areas for a few hours in the morning and evening. Children went to school at one-room, one-teacher elementary schools. Until after World War II, a student wishing to obtain a high-school education was forced to board in Key West.

The Florida land boom of 1924 to 1926 reached into the Keys. Land prices soared, large parcels of virgin Keys acreage were subdivided, and real estate sales were brisk. Prices ranged from $1,000 to as much as $25,000 an acre for prime waterfront locations. In 1926, the bubble burst and land values took a steep dive, not to recover until after the war.

Motorcade inaugurating the first Overseas Highway, January 22, 1928 (courtesy of Monroe County Public Library)

Construction of the highway provided jobs for a number of Keys natives. After it was completed, some found continued employment in road maintenance or as ferry crewmen. As service stations and tourist facilities opened, new jobs became available, and subsistence farmers gradually abandoned their fields.

Initially, there was a forty-mile gap in the Overseas Highway between No Name Key and Lower Matecumbe Key. Three ferries shuttled cars across the gap until, in 1930, workers completed a road across Key Vaca and Grassy Key. This cut the ferry service to two fourteen-mile crossings: No Name Key to Knight Key and Grassy Key to Lower Matecumbe Key.

Overshadowing all other events in the Keys in the 1920s and 1930s was the Labor Day hurricane of 1935, one of the most powerful storms to strike the United States in modern times. The eye of the storm, with winds of 200-plus miles per hour, passed over the Matecumbe keys. What the winds did not destroy, fifteen-foot-high walls of water, racing across the islands, swept away. When it was over, more than 400 were dead. Most of them were World War I veterans employed by the WPA to build highway bridges and housed in tents and temporary barracks on Lower Matecumbe.

But also lost were approximately 160 Keys natives. Old-time Bahamian pioneer families like the Russells and the Parkers were virtually wiped out.

Also gone with the winds and waves were large sections of railroad track and roadbed in the upper Keys. The railroad bridges withstood the onslaught intact and the railroad could have been rebuilt. But the Flagler railroad system was in receivership and the bankruptcy court ruled against rebuilding. The right of way was sold to the Overseas Toll Bridge Commission and, in November 1936, workers began building a new overseas highway across the railroad bridges and roadbed. The new highway opened in March 1938 and, for the first time, it became possible to drive from Key West to Miami without a ferry ride.

The effects of the Depression were felt throughout the Keys, but most heavily in the city of Key West. By 1934, 80 percent of its 11,000 residents were on relief and the city was bankrupt. The Federal Emergency Relief Administration took over government of the city and inaugurated a program to transform the town into a tourist mecca.

In 1935, before the hurricane, the rural Keys population had reached approximately 900. Following a sharp post-hurricane drop, the numbers did not reach that figure again until after the beginning of World War II. Farming and fishing were still the major occupations in 1935, but transportation and tourist-oriented occupations were not far behind.

A few enterprising businessmen had already started projects to bring tourists to the rural Keys when the Depression began. The posh Long Key Fishing Camp continued operating until it was destroyed in the 1935 hurricane. Another millionaires' fishing resort, the Matecumbe Club, opened in 1924 only to be washed out to sea by the same hurricane. Undaunted by these disasters, C. Irving Wright built a luxury fishing resort on Sugarloaf Key with the romantic name "Pirates Cove." The resort, designed to attract wives as well as their fishermen husbands, opened in 1930. Its amenities for seventy guests included a lodge, dining hall, cabins, swimming pool, and paddle-tennis courts. The guest register listed wealthy sportsmen, famous writers, business tycoons, and even royalty.

As the 1930s progressed, smaller and less-pretentious fishing camps, tourist cabins, and hotels sprang into existence up and down the Keys. In 1939, real estate developer Richter C. Perky converted his private estate on

Sugarloaf Key to a resort named Perky Lodge. The story of Perky's ventures in the Keys, including his famous bat tower, follows in this chapter. By the beginning of World War II, tourism was well established as the direction for the future of the rural Keys.

Big Pine Shark Skinners — Leather and Oil from the Sea

Joe Whalton recalls that a visit to the shark camp on Big Pine Key was a favorite activity during his boyhood stays at a nearby family vacation retreat. "The place was close enough that we could see it and smell it — there were times it was really ripe. A whole bunch of us would pole or scull a boat up to watch them skin the sharks. Sometimes we got in the way, but the workers, most of them blacks, were real nice. They would never holler at us and they got a kick out of watching us dig out the shark eyeballs."

The Big Pine Key shark facility was built in 1923 by Hydenoil Products to catch and process sharks for various commercial uses. The company's name was derived from the two principal products: hides for sharkskin leather, and oil from the liver for use as a medicine.

The camp was located on the eastern shore of Big Pine Key about two miles north of the railroad bridge. When it opened, it employed about twenty-five men and operated six shark-fishing boats. In addition to a 400-foot pier extending into the deeper water of Bogie Channel, there was a marine railway for hauling the carcasses ashore, large kettles for boiling livers under a palmetto-roofed shed, racks for drying and repairing nets, and various office and storage buildings.

The sharks were caught in huge nets, up to 600 feet in length and fifteen feet in depth, with a nine-inch square mesh. The tops of the nets were buoyed with wood floats, and the bottoms were held down with lead weights.

When a shark hit the net, it would continue to charge ahead and thrash about furiously. During its struggles, the net cords would slip behind the shark's gills and interfere with its breathing. Most of the sharks would be dead from drowning when the nets were hauled. One exception was the sawfish, a more lethargic type of shark, which usually had to be clubbed to death, while taking care to avoid the wildly swinging saw. Some of the monsters weighed close to 1,000 pounds and reached nearly twenty feet in length, so getting them aboard, even with the aid of block and tackle, was a herculean task.

The species most often caught were leopard, dusky, hammerhead, nurse, sand, and sawfish sharks. Of these, the sawfish was the most valuable because it yielded the largest hides and had the best vitamins in its liver. In the first four months of operation, Hydenoil boats took 5,000 sharks. Single-day catches of fifty sharks were common, and on one occasion, the catch approached 100. In that first year, one of the boats caught an eighteen-foot lemon shark weighing 901 pounds. By 1930, close to 100 sharks averaging seven feet in length were being caught every day.

The fishermen found all sorts of unusual objects when they cut the shark's stomachs open, among them a barrel of salt pork and the entire hindquarters of a Key deer. But the most grisly find was made by Capt. W. E. Young, a shark fishing expert, who wrote a book entitled *Shark, Shark!*

While in the employ of Hydenoil in January 1923, Young caught a twelve-foot brown shark off Big Pine Key. Upon slicing open the belly, he found a human arm and hand and a piece of blue serge cloth. From immediate inquiries, he learned that an Aeromarine Airways seaplane had crashed in the sea about twenty miles from Havana the day before he caught the shark. A lifeboat from the railroad-car ferry *Henry M. Fagler* had managed to rescue the pilot, the mechanic, and four passengers, but four other passengers were not recovered. The piece of cloth identified the shark's victim as one of the missing passengers.

Upon returning to Big Pine Key, the fishermen offloaded the sharks with a big crane at the end of the pier. Several men rapidly cut away the hides with sharp knives. They loaded the carcasses and hides onto a flat car riding on a marine railway which was then winched ashore to the processing facility.

In February 1923, Hydenoil announced that it had developed a new apparatus which greatly reduced skinning time. The workers lowered a shark into the device, cut the hide partially away near the head and clamped it, and then literally hoisted the shark out of its skin. Other processing improvements that year cut the curing time for fresh hides from thirty days to twenty four hours.

The facility shipped the dried hides north via the Overseas Railroad for tanning and processing into leather. Shark leather is stronger than most leathers, soft and pliable, takes dye readily, and can be used to make almost any article made of leather, including shoes.

After the sharks were offloaded, the boat crews took their nets ashore and spread them out on racks for drying and repairing. There was always damage, particularly from sawfish that would slash great holes in the nets. One man kept busy continuously making repairs.

Shark livers were cut out and reduced to oil in large double boilers under a shed. Approximately seventy-five percent of the liver was oil. Rich in vitamins, it was sold as a medicine. Spongers also used the oil to calm and clarify the water surface on breezy days.

A couple who visited the camp in 1926 observed the operations and commented that the place was kept quite clean considering the nature of the work. They saw a number of men skinning sharks with knives, which would indicate that the marvelous skinning apparatus was no longer in use. Other men cut the white shark meat into large slabs which were then salt-ed, compressed in heavy presses, and laid out to dry on a long chicken-wire fence. Shark fins found a ready market in the Orient, where they were con-sidered a great delicacy.

Hardly any part of the shark was wasted. When boiled, the heads yielded a large quantity of glue. Insulin for treating diabetes was obtained from the pancreas. The teeth and jaws were sold as curios, and the verte-brae were made into walking canes. Harold Terry of Big Pine Key remem-bers seeing shark skeletons spread out over an acre of cleared land to dry, after which they were ground up to make fertilizer.

Even the eyeballs had a use. Joe Whalton remembers how, as a very young boy, he watched the older children, including his cousin Doris Hart, take out the eyeballs. Doris described the procedure this way: "Remember the piles of shark? We used to get up on top and cut the eyes out. You would stick two fingers right in under the eyeball and lift it up and take it out. It was in a jelly and you'd put it in your little bucket of water and get all that jelly off, and there was a beautiful, clear crystal lens. You'd take a piece of cotton with you in a little bandaid can, and put your little eyeballs down in the cotton so they wouldn't hit each other and crack (invariably all of mine cracked), but if they didn't crack or cloud, they made beautiful men's stick pins."

Big Pine Key shark camp scenes circa 1930 (Courtesy of John Sands)

In June 1930, Hydenoil, with seven shark fishing boats and sixty employees, announced plans to expand the Big Pine operations by increasing the fleet to twenty boats. Some of the new boats were to be "run" boats that would transport the daily catch back to camp.

However, just two months later, thirty-six employees quit working because they had not been paid in seven weeks. In November, operations were underway again; and in December, a 1,752-pound mackerel shark, the largest shark yet caught, was brought into Big Pine Key.

Sometime in 1931, the camp shut down operations again, presumably because of a shortage of financing. A ray of hope appeared in October, when a new president of Hydenoil announced he would come down to inspect the Big Pine Key facility. Less than a month later, though, acting on a complaint by the local manager that the company owed him $3,000, mostly in back wages, the sheriff seized all the company's assets on Big Pine.

There were other shark-fishing enterprises in the Keys after the Big Pine Key camp closed in 1931, but none of them rivaled the Big Pine Key operation in size or longevity. With its closure, another Keys industry, like pineapple growing and sponge farming before it, was on its way into history.

Richter Perky – The Bats Didn't Come to Sugarloaf

Perky, a place that faded into obscurity more than fifty years ago, still occasionally appears on maps of the Florida Keys. Located on Sugarloaf Key near the present-day site of the Sugarloaf Lodge resort, it was once the vacation retreat of the largest private landowner in the Florida Keys. It was also the scene of failed efforts to revive artificial cultivation of sponges, to eradicate mosquitoes with bats, and to develop a luxury fishing resort.

In the mid-1930s, Perky was the home of Fred Johnson, the settlement's postmaster, general superintendent, and deputy sheriff. This is the story of Perky, the Johnson family, and life on Sugarloaf Key in the 1930s.

In 1925, a wealthy Florida real-estate salesman, Richter C. Perky, purchased the Chase brothers' sponge-farming property (see Charles Chase, Chapter 7). Perky eventually owned some 23,000 acres in the Keys, more than any other individual or company except the Florida East Coast Railway. Sugarloaf Key was to be a vacation retreat from his home office in Miami. He also planned to try his hand at artificial cultivation of sponges.

When Perky first acquired the Sugarloaf property, the only means of reaching it was by small boat or train from Miami or Key West. However, construction of the first overseas highway from Miami to Key West had begun and, by 1927, its narrow roadway and wooden bridges had reached Sugarloaf Key. Unfortunately for Perky, the road ran along the southern shore of Sugarloaf, three miles south of his place.

In 1928, Perky hired Fred Johnson, of Key West, to be caretaker and general superintendent of construction for his Sugarloaf property. This was the beginning of a relationship between the two men which, over the next twelve years, ripened into mutual respect and warm friendship.

Work now began in earnest to create a private vacation and fishing retreat for Perky and his wealthy friends. One of Fred's first jobs was to clear a rough trail for automobile access to the overseas highway on the southern shoreline. Subsequently, Perky advanced $15,000 to Monroe County to fill and grade the road which today is called Sugarloaf Boulevard.

The Bat Tower at Perky, Sugarloaf Key; inscription at base reads: "Dedicated to good health at Perky, Florida by Mr. and Mrs. R. C. Perky, March 15, 1929." (courtesy of Florida State Archives)

The biggest drawback to Perky's vacation paradise was the mosquito population. Fred said it was so bad at times that you could rake the mosquitoes off your arms in piles.

During trips to Texas in connection with his oil well interests, Perky heard of towers built to house bats which in turn would devour all the mosquitoes in the surrounding area. After investigating and becoming convinced of the feasibility of the idea, he directed Fred to build a bat tower at Sugarloaf.

In five months, with three workers, Fred completed the fifty-foot-high tower. He then installed and activated the bait that was supposed to attract bats to the tower. However, despite the awful stench that rose from the bait, no bats came and the mosquitoes remained.

Many other projects were underway at what, in 1929, officially became Perky, Florida, with its own post office. Under Fred's supervision, a generating plant, two thirty-five-foot water towers, and a large residence for Perky were built to provide modern conveniences and accommodations.

Much of the facilities and equipment from the Chase brothers' sponge-growing days remained, and Perky was hopeful that he could succeed where they had failed. With his influence, he was able to get the Florida Legislature to pass an act granting him the same exclusive rights given the Chase brothers to grow and harvest sponges in the Sugarloaf sounds.

Fred began planting sponges using the same methods as in the earlier effort. Natural sponges were cut into small pieces about the size of an egg, wired to concrete disks, and tossed into the shallow waters of the sounds. Fred soon discovered that the railroad embankments had so restricted water flow in and out of the southern portion of the upper sound that it was devoid of marine life, and sponges would not grow there. To correct the problem, Fred, with the aid of a dragline barge and dynamite, dredged a canal from the sound out to open water. The same canal is used today by boaters from Sugarloaf Shores to get to Hawk Channel and the reef.

As in the Chase brothers' days, local spongers refused to recognize anyone's exclusive rights to sponge gathering in the Sugarloaf sounds. Signs were posted, intruders were warned, and Fred was appointed a deputy sheriff with authority to arrest poachers – but still they came. In 1930, Fred finally arrested one and took him to Key West. There, a justice of the peace freed the sponger and declared the 1929 legislative act to be unconstitutional.

It was a difficult situation for Fred. His wife and children still lived in Key West and he came down to be with them on weekends. However, as Perky's representative and enforcer of his sponge rights, he was not well received by the local spongers.

The following year, 1931, the state's Internal Improvement Board canceled the lease which gave Perky exclusive access to the sounds and a judge dismissed Perky's petition to bar local spongers from using the sounds. Perky appealed the decision to the State Supreme Court, but three years passed before a ruling in his favor was handed down. In the meantime, sponge planting was halted and never again resumed. Once again, no artificially cultivated sponges were harvested, except by poachers.

Even in the 1930s, Sugarloaf Key was an isolated, sparsely populated place. Perky spent most of his time at his home and office in Miami, coming to Sugarloaf only for short periods of relaxation and fishing. The only year-round residents at Perky were Fred, until his family joined him in 1936, and a black couple remembered as Jim and Maggie.

The liveliest place on the Key was Pirates Cove, a fishing resort with accommodations for seventy guests on the eastern shore a short distance south of the railroad bridge. The only other residents of the island were the railroad section foreman and his crew, one or two farmers, and a black man who made charcoal.

During Fred's first years at Perky, his wife Mary and the children remained in Key West. Fred went home on weekends, but during school vacations his family came to Perky. Fred remodeled and enlarged the home of the former owner, Charles Chase, to accommodate his family, which by 1932 had grown to five children. The two-story stilt house had a large screened porch surrounding the upper story. A unique feature was a double-door entrance to the porch where mosquitoes were scraped or sprayed off before entering.

With the failure of the bat tower experiment, mosquitoes continued to make life miserable at Perky at times. Fred did what he could by digging drainage ditches, putting oil-soaked sponges in ponds he could not drain, and lighting smudge fires, but with little effect.

While the adults suffered, the children were not particularly bothered. Fred Jr. recalls, "I would have them all over me, but I just brushed them off." A favorite pastime of the children was to press their hands against the porch screen. The mosquitoes would gather so quickly and thickly on the outside that images of their hands would remain when they withdrew them.

In 1936, Mary and the children moved to Perky to stay year round. The children were delighted; to them, Perky was a fishing, swimming, and boating paradise. To their mother, however, it was an isolated outpost of civilization, devoid of all adult female companionship.

Even her husband's company was limited, particularly when Perky was in residence. If he had a group of guests, as he often did, Fred had to take them out fishing and look after their needs. If Perky was alone, he usually slept all day and then expected Fred, who had worked all day, to talk with him into the wee hours of the morning. But Fred did not complain. He was a hard-working, loyal employee, even telling his children they could not sell the spiny lobster they caught because "they belonged to Mr. Perky."

On long weekends, the Johnson family drove to Key West in Perky's Model A Ford to stock up on groceries. The twenty-mile trip on the first overseas roadway, over the narrow wooden bridges and around the blind curve on Saddlebunch Key known as "Deadman's Curve," took about an hour. When the traffic was heavy, they might meet as many as five or six other cars along the way.

Despite its isolation, life on Perky was not uncivilized. A power plant supplied electricity for lights and for pumping water into the two water towers. Two large cisterns stored all the fresh water needed by the few residents.

Even telephone service became available. The only telephone line in the Keys outside of Key West belonged to the U.S. Coast Guard and was used for communicating with the lighthouses. In order to get on the line, Perky donated a right-of-way across his property on Sugarloaf for the line connecting to the underwater cable to American Shoals lighthouse. Fred recalled that he used to ring up American Shoals when there was a big prize fight on and place the receiver next to his radio so the lighthouse keepers could listen to the blow-by-blow.

As postmaster for Perky, one of Fred's duties was to get the mail off the train. There was a flag stop where Sugarloaf Lodge is today. The train would stop if there were passengers waiting to board or wanting to get off, but it would not stop for the mail transfer. An ingenious method was used.

The outgoing mail bag was suspended from an overhanging arm alongside the track. As the train approached, a long pole on a pivot with a hook caught the bag, swung it aboard, and, in the process, pulled it free of the quick-release attachment. Simultaneously, the mailman kicked the Perky mail bag off the train and onto the platform.

Three of the Johnson children, Fred Jr., Betty, and Buddy, were of school age when the family moved to Perky. A one-room, two-outhouse school was located on the eastern side of Big Pine Key a short distance north of the railroad. A single teacher taught grades one through six to a student body of about a dozen pupils.

The school bus picked up the Johnson children about 7:30 in the morning and did not arrive home again until 5:00 in the evening. The driver was Mizpah Saunders. When Mizpah was a young girl, her father, Robert Watson, had homesteaded on Big Pine Key in the area known today as Watson's Hammock.

Mary Johnson always felt uneasy during the long day her children were away at school. She worried about the narrow bridges, some with missing guardrails, and the possibility that the bus might have a flat tire or a blowout and plunge into the water.

Mizpah was also concerned, but about a different problem. The children liked to hang out the windows to look for birds and animals, and she was afraid they would be hit by an overhanging tree branch or a passing car. She told them that one day the bus rolled over a rattlesnake and the snake was thrown up into the bus through an open window. After that, the windows stayed rolled up.

After school and on the weekends, fishing was the children's favorite sport. Using lobster for bait, they would fish off the end of the long stone dock their father had built. The older children were allowed to go out in a skiff kept in the "back" sound. Their father had also enclosed a large shallow water area at the shore end of the dock and had made a small beach. Here the children could swim without their mother being concerned.

The Johnsons kept a cow, chickens, and ducks, and each child had his own pet duckling. They were fascinated by the wild animals and birds in the area, but were cautioned not to wander into the bushes because of the

Fred Johnson, Manager of the Perky Estate, and his wife Mary in their later years (courtesy of their daughter Sylvia Johnson Torres)

rattlesnakes. Sometimes raccoons would fall asleep in the date palms by the house after gorging themselves on dates. In the morning, the children would poke them out of the tree with a long stick, catch them in a sheet and keep them as pets. On very hot days, they would climb to the top of the lookout tower (built to spot sponge poachers) to catch a little breeze and laze in the shade.

The 1930s Depression greatly reduced Perky's land sales and his cash flow. With the opening of the new overseas highway (using the railroad-right-of-way and bridges) in 1938, Perky decided to convert his 365-acre private retreat into a luxury fishing resort. Under Fred's supervision, the existing buildings were remodeled and new buildings were added to provide sleeping, dining, and recreational facilities.

In March 1939, Perky Lodge opened to the public. The brochure boasted that the lobby, dining room and taproom were paneled in pecky cypress and that every room had innerspring mattresses and hot and cold running water.

However, the days of Perky Lodge were numbered. The following year, with Fred at his bedside in Miami, Perky died, as Fred said, "land poor." The trustees of the estate had no money to pay Fred his back wages, then five or six months in arrears. Fred reluctantly left his home and job of fourteen years and took a position at the Navy yard in Key West. Mary had a somewhat different attitude toward the change. As she put it, "My happiest moment was the day Fred left Perky."

With the death of its founder, Perky quickly faded into obscurity. In 1943, two of the largest buildings, Perky's and Johnson's former residences, were destroyed by fire. The bat tower, now designated a historic landmark, still stands, a curious reminder of a futile experiment and a forgotten time.

145

Bibliography

Chapter 1

Carr, Robert S. "Prehistoric Settlement of the Florida Keys." *The Monroe County Environmental Story.* Jeannette Gato, Editor-in-Chief and Dan Gallagher, Ph.D., Executive Editor. Big Pine Key: Monroe County Environmental Education Task Force, 1991.

Charlevoix's Louisiana. Selections from the *History and the Journal* by Pierre F. X. de Charlevoix. Edited by Charles E. O'Neill. Baton Rouge: Louisiana State University Press, 1977.

Fontaneda, Do. d'Escalante. *Memoir of Do. d'Escalante Fontaneda Respecting Florida Written in Spain, About the Year 1575.* Translated by Buckingham Smith. Annotated by David O. True. Coral Gables: Glades House, 1944.

Goggin, John M., and Frank H. Sommer. "Excavations on Upper Matecumbe Key, Florida." *Yale University Publications in Anthropology.* Nos. 41 and 42. New Haven: Yale University Press, 1949.

Missions to the Calusa. Edited and translated by John H. Hann. Gainesville: University of Florida Press, 1991.

Chapter 2

Arnade, Charles W. "Florida Keys: English or Spanish in 1763?" *Tequesta.* No. 15 (1955): 41-53. Miami: Historical Association of Southern Florida, 1955.

Fanning, David. *The Narrative of Colonel David Fanning.* Edited with an introduction and notes by Lindley S. Butler. Charleston, S.C.: Tradd St. Press, 1981.

Romans, Bernard. *A Concise Natural History of East and West Florida.* Facsimile reproduction of the 1775 edition. Gainesville: University of Florida Press, 1962.

Chapter 3

Brigham, Florence S. "Key Vaca Parts I and II." *Tequesta.* No. 17 (1957): 47–67 and No. 18 (1958): 23–75. Miami: Historical Association of Southern Florida, 1957 and 1958.

Browne, Jefferson B. *Key West the Old and the New*. Facsimile reproduction of the 1912 edition. Gainesville: University of Florida Press, 1973.

Letters, depositions, and other documents in the Joshua Appleby file. Vault A. Box 129. Folder 5. Newport Historical Society.

Porter, David. Letters to the Secretary of the Navy, various dates in 1823. *Territorial Papers of the U.S. Vol. XXVII, The Territory of Florida, 1821–1823*. Washington, D.C.: U.S. Government Printing Office, 1956.

Schene, Michael G. "History of Indian Key." Miscellaneous Project Report Series No. 8. Tallahassee: Bureau of Historic Sites and Properties; Division of Archives, History, and Records Management; Florida Department of State, 1973.

Chapter 4

Buker, George E. *Swamp Sailors*. Gainesville: The University Presses of Florida, 1975.

Dodd, Dorothy. "Jacob Housman of Indian Key." *Tequesta*. No. 8 (1948): 3–19. Miami: Historical Association of Southern Florida, 1948.

Howe, Charles. "A Letter from Indian Key, 1840." *The Florida Historical Quarterly*. Vol. 20 No. 2 (1941): 197–202. Tampa, Fla.: The Florida Historical Society, 1941.

Key West Enquirer. News items, various dates in 1836.

"Lighthouse Records." Federal Writers Program. Microfilm. Monroe County Public Library, Key West.

Perrine, Henry. "Random Records of Tropical Florida." *Tequesta*. No. 11 (1951): 51–62. Miami: Historical Association of Southern Florida, 1951.

Perrine, Henry E. *A True Story of Some Eventful Years in Grandpa's Life*. Buffalo, N.Y.: E. H. Hutchinson, 1885.

"Petition and Remonstrance to Congress by Inhabitants of Monroe County. March 1, 1836, and No Date, 1836." *Territorial Papers of the U.S. Vol. XV, The Territory of Florida 1834–1839*. Washington, D.C.:

U.S. Government Printing Office, 1960.

Sturtevant, William C. "Chakaika and the 'Spanish Indians'" *Tequesta*. No. 13 (1953): 35–73. Miami: Historical Association of Southern Florida, 1953.

Walker, Hester Perrine. "Massacre at Indian Key, August 7, 1840, and the Death of Doctor Henry Perrine." *The Florida Historical Quarterly*. Vol. 5 (1948): 3–19. Tampa, Fla.: The Florida Historical Society, 1948.

Whalton, John. Letters to the Collector of Revenue, Key West and the Commissioner of the Revenue, Washington, 1824–1828 from the collection of Mrs. J. C. Whalton.

Chapter 5

Census of the United States. Florida, Dade and Monroe Counties, 1850 and 1860.

Certificate of permission to settle issued to Henry Geiger under the provisions of the Armed Occupation Act, July 19, 1843. Monroe County Deed Book.

Diary/Sketchbook of an Unknown Boston Artist, 1851. In the collection of The Winterthur Library, Winterthur, Delaware.

"The Florida Keys." *Putnam's Monthly*. Vol. 8, December 1856: 563–564.

Hackley, William R. Key West attorney. Diary, 1828–1857.

Lytton, Eugene R. "The Honorable Squire Temple Pent, Sr." Privately published, 1992.

Parks, Pat. "Visiting Along the Lower Keys–Two Tragedies." *The Key West Citizen*. September 4, 1969.

Reports of the Superintendent of the United States Coast Survey during the period 1849 to 1856.

Chapter 6

Census of the United States. Florida, Monroe County, 1870, 1880, and 1900.

Citizenship Certificate, Homestead Proof, Death Certificate, and other documents concerning Nicholas Matcovich from the collection of his great-granddaughter, Patricia B. Warren, of Miami, Florida.

Fairchild, David G. *The World Was My Garden*. New York: Scribner, 1938.

"Florida–A Pamphlet Descriptive of Its History, Topography, Climate, Soil, Etc. 1904." Florida Department of Agriculture, 1904.

"Fruit Farming on the Keys. A Visit to the Matcovich Plantation on No Name Key." *The Key West Citizen.* October 22, 1908.

Kennedy, Stetson. "Charcoal Kilns on the Florida Keys." *Literary Florida.* December 1939: 3–6.

Monroe, Kirk. "Pineapples of the Florida Keys." *Harper's Weekly.* August 22, 1896: 825–826.

Chapter 7

Bow, Lily Lawrence. "Cudjoe" (a poem). *Redland District News.* April 5, 1938.

Census of the United States. Florida, Monroe County, 1910 and 1920.

Chase, Charles W. Interview by Mrs. J. C. Whalton, 1973. Tape recording at Monroe County Public Library, Key West.

Chase, Charles W. Letters to Mr. and Mrs. J. C. Whalton, various dates in 1971 and 1972, from the collection of Mrs. J. C. Whalton.

Key, Frederick. Interview by the author, 1989.

Letters, newspaper clippings, and other documents concerning Lily Lawrence Bow from the collection of her granddaughter, Mary Bow.

Parks, Pat. *The Railroad that Died at Sea.* Key West, Fla: The Langley Press, 1968.

Roberts, Lillian Spencer. Interview by the author, 1988.

Chapter 8

Hopkins, Alice. "The Development of the Overseas Highway." *Tequesta.* No. 46 (1986): 51–52. Miami: The Historical Association of Southern Florida, 1986.

Johnson, Fred. Interview by Betty Bruce, July 18, 1967. Tape recording at the Monroe County Public Library, Key West.

Johnson, Fred. Interview by Wright Langley, 1980. Tape recording at the Monroe County Public Library, Key West.

Johnson, Mary; Johnson, Fred Jr.; Torres, Sylvia Johnson. Interview by the author, 1989.

"Little Talks About Tropical Things." *Tropic Magazine.* February 1926: 153–177. Miami: The Tropic Publishing Co., 1926.

Whalton, Joseph C. Interview by the author, 1989.

Index

Illustrations are indicated in boldface type.

If you enjoyed this book, here are some other books from Pineapple Press on related topics. For a complete catalog, write to Pineapple Press, P.O. Box 3899, Sarasota, FL 34230, or call (800) 746-3275.

History/Biography/Folklore

African Americans in Florida by Maxine D. Jones and Kevin M. McCarthy. Profiles of African-American writers, politicians, educators, sportsmen, and others in brief essays covering over four centuries. Suitable for school-age readers. Teacher's manual available.

Classic Cracker by Ronald W. Haase. A study of Florida's wood-frame vernacular architecture that traces the historical development of the regional building style that offered human comfort in Florida's environment.

Dreamers, Schemers, and Scalawags: The Florida Chronicles Vol. 1 by Stuart B. McIver. Engaging character sketches of unusual characters who made Florida their home: includes storytellers, tycoons, moviemakers, and more.

The Everglades: River of Grass by Marjory Stoneman Douglas. A treasured classic of nature writing in its fifth printing, this is the book that launched the fight to preserve the Florida Everglades

Florida Place Names by Allen Morris. A unique reference that describes the origin and meaning of the name of every county and incorporated city in Florida as well as hundreds of others. Includes a hundred black and white photos edited by Joan Perry Morris, curator of the Florida State Archives.

Florida Portrait by Jerrell Shofner. A beautiful volume of words and pictures that traces the history of Florida from the Paleoindians to the rampant growth of the twentieth century.

The Florida Reader edited by Maurice O'Sullivan and Jack Lane. A historical and literary anthology of visions of paradise from a diverse gathering of voices, including Ralph Waldo Emerson, Marjorie Kinnan Rawlings, and Harry Crews.

Florida's First People by Robin C. Brown. A clearly written and richly illustrated volume that brings to life the first humans who entered Florida 12,000 years ago.

Florida's Past (3 volumes) by Gene Burnett. A popular collection of essays about the people and events that shaped the state.

Hemingway's Key West by Stuart B. McIver. A rousing, true-to-life portrait of Hemingway the man and the writer during the 1930s when he and his family lived in Key West.

The Houses of Key West by Alex Caemmerer. A full-color examination of Key West's architectural treasure trove.

Legends of the Seminoles by Betty Mae Jumper with Peter Gallagher. Tales told around the campfires to Seminole children, now written down for the first time. Each story illustrated with an original painting by Guy LaBree.

Key Biscayne: A History of Miami's Tropical Island and the Cape Florida Lighthouse by Joan Gill Blank. In the series *Florida's History through Its Places,* this volume ties together the island's unique geography, environment, and history.

Menéndez by Albert Manucy. A biography of the founder of St. Augustine.

Murder in the Tropics: The Florida Chronicles Vol. 2 by Stuart B. McIver. A compelling collection of true crime in paradise.

Shipwrecks of Florida by Steven D. Singer. A comprehensive reference book arranged chronologically within geographical sections of the state. For serious divers and curious readers alike.

Spanish Pathways in Florida edited by Ann L. Henderson and Gary R. Mormino. Essays, in both Spanish and English, on the influence of the Spanish in Florida, from the first explorers to the latest Hispanic migrations into Miami.

The Spanish Treasure Fleets by Timothy Walton. The rise and fall of Spain's economic world dominance based on the precious metals plundered from the New World.

Thirty Florida Shipwrecks by Kevin M. McCarthy. The best shipwreck stories, from young Fontaneda, wrecked in 1545 and held captive by Indians for 17 years, to the Coast Guard cutter *Bibb*, sunk off Key Largo in 1978. Illustrated by William Trotter.

Twenty Florida Pirates by Kevin M. McCarthy. Tales of the most notorious Florida pirates, from the 1500s to the present day. Illustrations by William Trotter.

Historical Fiction

A Land Remembered by Patrick Smith. A sweeping saga of three generations of Florida settlers. Winner of the Florida Historical Society's Tebeau Prize as the Most Outstanding Florida Historical Novel.

Guns of the Palmetto Plains by Rick Tonyan. An action-packed Cracker Western that plunges the reader into the last agonizing years of the Civil War. Snake-filled swamps, Yankee raiders, and vicious outlaws block the trails between Florida and the rest of the Confederacy, leaving the untamed peninsula to the heroes and the gunslingers.

Riders of the Suwannee by Lee Gramling. Tate Barkley returns to Florida in the 1870s from the Western frontier, only to find out that his gunfighting days are not over. When Tate pulls out his Winchester, you can count on the kind of action that will keep pages turning right on to the all-out fight at the end of this Cracker Western.

Thunder on the St. Johns by Lee Gramling. The vast unsettled lands of Florida in the 1850s are home to honest hard-working homesteaders and greedy violent power mongers. Which kind of folk will prevail in this gripping Cracker Western?

Trail from St. Augustine by Lee Gramling. In this Cracker Western a fur trapper and a young woman indentured by a powerful tyrant are pursued across the Florida wilderness to a showdown on the windswept sands of the Florida Gulf coast.